D0893647

MAMMALS

Britannica Illustrated Science Library

Encyclopædia Britannica, Inc.

Chicago ▪ London ▪ New Delhi ▪ Paris ▪ Seoul ▪ Sydney ▪ Taipei ▪ Tokyo

Britannica Illustrated Science Library

© 2008 Editorial Sol 90
All rights reserved.

Idea and Concept of This Work: Editorial Sol 90

Project Management: Fabián Cassan

Photo Credits: Corbis, ESA, Getty Images, Bryan Mullennix—Riser/Getty Images, Graphic News, NASA, National Geographic, Science Photo Library

Illustrators: Guido Arroyo, Pablo Aschei, Gustavo J. Caironi, Hernán Cañellas, Leonardo César, José Luis Corsetti, Vanina Farías, Manrique Fernández Buente, Joana Garrido, Celina Hilbert, Jorge Ivanovich, Isidro López, Diego Martín, Jorge Martínez, Marco Menco, Marcelo Morán, Ala de Mosca, Diego Mourelos, Pablo Palastro, Eduardo Pérez, Javier Pérez, Ariel Piroyansky, Fernando Ramallo, Ariel Roldán, Marcel Socías, Néstor Taylor, Trebol Animation, Juan Venegas, Constanza Vicco, Coralia Vignau, Gustavo Yamin, 3DN, 3DOM studio

Composition and Pre-press Services: Editorial Sol 90
Translation Services and Index: Publication Services, Inc.

Portions © 2008 Encyclopædia Britannica, Inc.
Encyclopædia Britannica, Britannica, and the thistle logo are registered trademarks of Encyclopædia Britannica, Inc.

Britannica Illustrated Science Library Staff

Editorial
Michael Levy, *Executive Editor, Core Editorial*
John Rafferty, *Associate Editor, Earth Sciences*
William L. Hosch, *Associate Editor, Mathematics and Computers*
Kara Rogers, *Associate Editor, Life Sciences*
Rob Curley, *Senior Editor, Science and Technology*
David Hayes, *Special Projects Editor*

Art and Composition
Steven N. Kapusta, *Director*
Carol A. Gaines, *Composition Supervisor*
Christine McCabe, *Senior Illustrator*

Media Acquisition
Kathy Nakamura, *Manager*

Copy Department
Sylvia Wallace, *Director*
Julian Ronning, *Supervisor*

Information Management and Retrieval
Sheila Vasich, *Information Architect*

Production Control
Marilyn L. Barton

Manufacturing
Kim Gerber, *Director*

Encyclopædia Britannica, Inc.

Jacob E. Safra, *Chairman of the Board*

Jorge Aguilar-Cauz, *President*

Michael Ross, *Senior Vice President, Corporate Development*

Dale H. Hoiberg, *Senior Vice President and Editor*

Marsha Mackenzie, *Director of Production*

International Standard Book Number (set):
978-1-59339-382-3
International Standard Book Number (volume):
978-1-59339-393-9
Britannica Illustrated Science Library: Mammals 2008

Printed in China

www.britannica.com

Mammals

Contents

WALES
Land of green meadows and gentle hills, Wales is famous the world over for the quality of its wool production.

Unique and Different

Mammals began to dominate the Earth about 65 million years ago. Without a doubt, modern humans are the most successful mammals—they occupy all the Earth's habitats! Their domestic coexistence with other species began barely 10,000 years BC, when human culture transitioned from a world of nomadic hunters and gatherers to a society based on agriculture. At that time, humans began to benefit from the meat and milk products of small mammals and to use large animals for labor. The first animals to be domesticated were sheep (about 9000 BC) in the Middle East. Pigs, cows, goats, and dogs followed. However, the great majority of mammal species continue, even today, to live in the wild.

There are 5,416 known mammal species distributed over different land and aquatic environments. Despite the characteristics that make them part of the same class, their diversity is such that the smallest of them, the shrew, may weigh only one tenth of an ounce (3 g), and the largest, the blue whale, can reach 160 tons. But their diversity is also evident in their adaptation to different environments. There are mammals that run and others that glide—some fly, and others jump, swim, or crawl. Most aquatic mammals have suppressed the development of hair or fur, replacing it with thick layers of fat. The rigors of low temperatures have made some animals—such as polar bears, dormice, and certain bats—exceptions to the vital law of homeothermy, as they spend the winter sunk in deep sleep to save energy.

Seals, dolphins, bats, and chimpanzees all have upper limbs with similar bones, but the environmental niche they occupy has made seals develop flippers, dolphins fins, bats wings, and chimpanzees arms. Thus from the polar tundra to the dense tropical jungle, through the deep oceans and high mountain lakes, the whole Earth has been populated by thousands of mammal species.

But this marvelous animal world has been disturbed by its most numerous species—humankind. Indiscriminate hunting, illegal trade, deforestation, urbanization, massive tourism, and pollution have left more than a thousand species (many of them mammals) endangered or vulnerable. However, science allows us to understand nature's many wonders, and it can help us respect the world's ecological balance. In this book, which includes dazzling photographs and illustrations, we invite you to discover many details of mammals' lives: their life cycles, their social lives, their special features, and their characteristics, from those of the greatest friend of them all, the dog, to the mysterious and solitary platypus. ●

Origin and Evolution

Polar bears are all-around athletes, as agile in the water as they are on land. Excellent swimmers, they move at a speed of 6 miles per hour (10 km/h) using a very rapid stroke. They can rest and even sleep in the water. Like all mammals, they have the ability to maintain a constant temperature. This allows them to tolerate the extreme cold

POLAR BEARS
Also called the white bear,
they are without a doubt
"Lords of the Arctic."
Nevertheless, they are on
the road to extinction.

of the Arctic ice. Here we will tell you many more things about the particular properties that distinguish mammals from the rest of the animals. Did you know that mammals appeared on Earth at almost the same time as dinosaurs? Since they were unable to compete with the large reptiles of the time, at first they were very small, similar to mice. Turn the page and you will discover many more things. ●

Millions of Years Ago . . .

The origin of mammals lies in the Triassic Period a little more than 220 million years ago when, in the course of terrestrial evolution, new groups of animals appeared. Their history can be reconstructed in broad outline through the study of fossils. Among them is the morganucodon, an animal of which we have found numerous remains. ●

Morganucodon

Clade	Mammaliaformes
Group	Synapsids
Subgroup	Triconodonts
Family	Cynodont
Genus	*Morganucodon*

Weight
1 to 1.8 ounces
(30-50 g)

6 inches (15 cm)

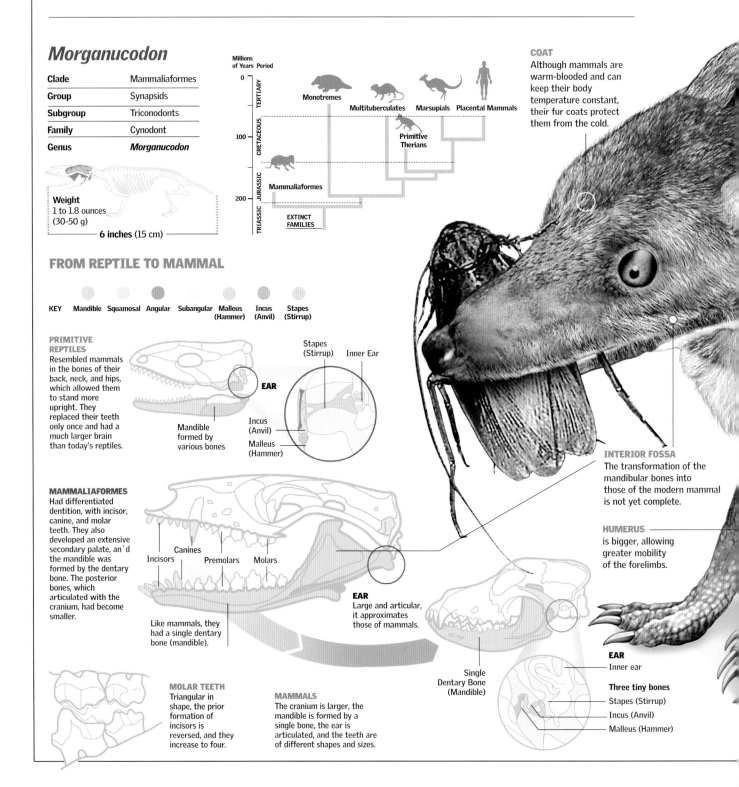

Millions of Years / Period

- TERTIARY
- CRETACEOUS
- JURASSIC
- TRIASSIC

Monotremes
Multituberculates
Marsupials
Placental Mammals
Primitive Therians
Mammaliaformes
EXTINCT FAMILIES

COAT
Although mammals are warm-blooded and can keep their body temperature constant, their fur coats protect them from the cold.

FROM REPTILE TO MAMMAL

KEY Mandible / Squamosal / Angular / Subangular / Malleus (Hammer) / Incus (Anvil) / Stapes (Stirrup)

PRIMITIVE REPTILES
Resembled mammals in the bones of their back, neck, and hips, which allowed them to stand more upright. They replaced their teeth only once and had a much larger brain than today's reptiles.

Mandible formed by various bones

EAR
Stapes (Stirrup)
Inner Ear
Incus (Anvil)
Malleus (Hammer)

MAMMALIAFORMES
Had differentiated dentition, with incisor, canine, and molar teeth. They also developed an extensive secondary palate, an`d the mandible was formed by the dentary bone. The posterior bones, which articulated with the cranium, had become smaller.

Incisors / Canines / Premolars / Molars

Like mammals, they had a single dentary bone (mandible).

EAR
Large and articular, it approximates those of mammals.

MOLAR TEETH
Triangular in shape, the prior formation of incisors is reversed, and they increase to four.

MAMMALS
The cranium is larger, the mandible is formed by a single bone, the ear is articulated, and the teeth are of different shapes and sizes.

Single Dentary Bone (Mandible)

INTERIOR FOSSA
The transformation of the mandibular bones into those of the modern mammal is not yet complete.

HUMERUS
is bigger, allowing greater mobility of the forelimbs.

EAR
Inner ear

Three tiny bones
Stapes (Stirrup)
Incus (Anvil)
Malleus (Hammer)

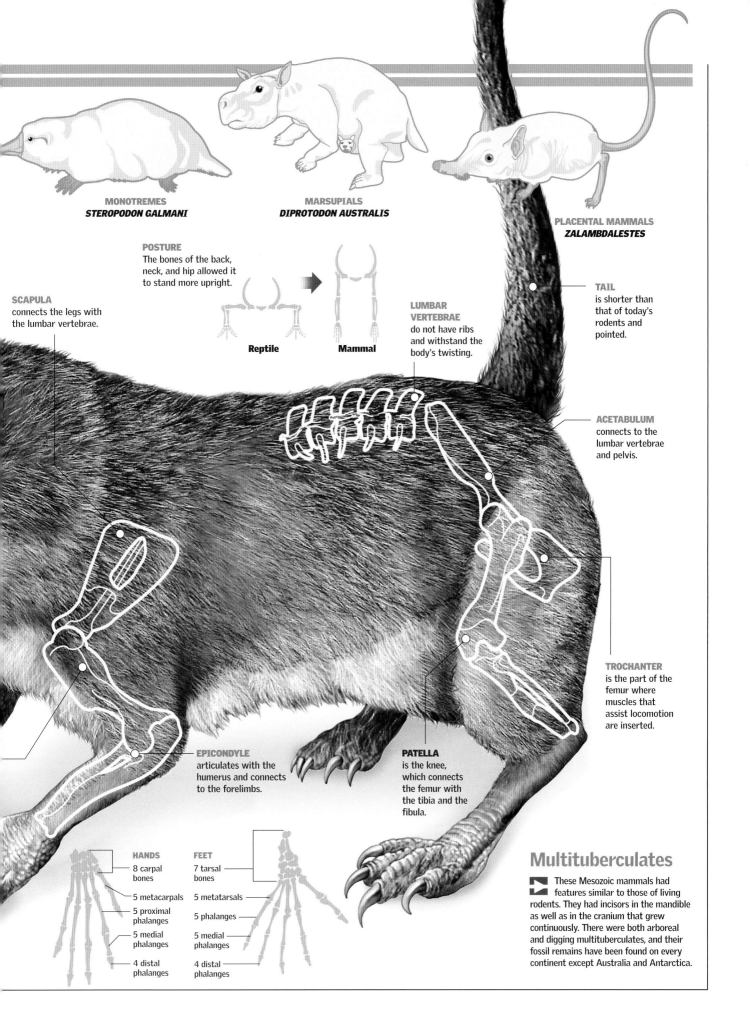

MONOTREMES
STEROPODON GALMANI

MARSUPIALS
DIPROTODON AUSTRALIS

PLACENTAL MAMMALS
ZALAMBDALESTES

POSTURE
The bones of the back, neck, and hip allowed it to stand more upright.

Reptile

Mammal

SCAPULA
connects the legs with the lumbar vertebrae.

LUMBAR VERTEBRAE
do not have ribs and withstand the body's twisting.

TAIL
is shorter than that of today's rodents and pointed.

ACETABULUM
connects to the lumbar vertebrae and pelvis.

TROCHANTER
is the part of the femur where muscles that assist locomotion are inserted.

EPICONDYLE
articulates with the humerus and connects to the forelimbs.

PATELLA
is the knee, which connects the femur with the tibia and the fibula.

HANDS
8 carpal bones
5 metacarpals
5 proximal phalanges
5 medial phalanges
4 distal phalanges

FEET
7 tarsal bones
5 metatarsals
5 phalanges
5 medial phalanges
4 distal phalanges

Multituberculates

These Mesozoic mammals had features similar to those of living rodents. They had incisors in the mandible as well as in the cranium that grew continuously. There were both arboreal and digging multituberculates, and their fossil remains have been found on every continent except Australia and Antarctica.

Names and Groups

The mammals class is divided into two subclasses: Prototheria, which lay eggs (like other classes such as birds), and Theria. The Theria, in turn, are divided into two infraclasses—Metatheria (marsupials), which grow to viability within a marsupium, or pouch, and Eutheria (placental mammals), whose offspring are born completely developed and who today represent the great majority of living mammal species, including humans. ●

Prototheria
Order Monotremata

Oviparous mammals (Monotremata) are the oldest of all known groups. It is believed that their origin could be independent from that of other mammals and that they descend directly from the Synapsid reptiles of the Triassic Period (more than 200 million years ago).

Monotremes are the only mammals that lay eggs. However, the shape of their craniums, the presence of hair, and, of course, mammary glands show that they belong to the mammal group. The mammary glands lack nipples, so the young have to lick milk from a tuft of hair.

The only living representatives of this order are echidnas and the platypus. The platypus is a unique species that, because of its similarity to birds, was impossible to classify zoologically for a long time.

ECHIDNA
Family Tachyglossidae
Also known as the "spiny anteater" because it feeds on ants and termites that it catches with its tongue. Its skin has hair and spines.

CURRENTLY
4
SPECIES KNOWN

HORNY BEAK
is used to rummage in riverbeds and mud in search of food.

FINS
Platypuses use their limbs to swim.

PLATYPUS
Family Ornithorhynchidae
A monotreme with semiaquatic habits. Its feet and tail possess membranes that make it palmate, which is useful for swimming. It feeds off any living thing it finds at the bottom of Australia's rivers or lakes by rummaging with its horny beak.

GEOGRAPHICALLY CONFINED
Platypuses and echidnas are found only in Oceania—the platypus only on Australia and the echidna (of which there are four species) also on the islands of Tasmania and New Guinea.

AUSTRALIA

Theria
Infraclass Metatheria

The principal characteristic of metatherias, or marsupials, is the way they reproduce and develop. They have a very short gestation period compared to other mammals (the longest is that of the giant gray kangaroo, only 38 days), which means that their newborn are not very developed but have bare skin and eyes and ears that are still in the formative stage—although they have a sense of smell, a mouth, and digestive and respiratory systems adequate for survival. When they are born, they crawl across their mother's abdomen in search of her mammary glands. Kangaroo offspring climb to the edge of the mother's pouch (marsupium). They then crawl in and affix themselves to one of the mammary glands, from which they feed until they complete development and leave the pouch.

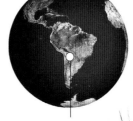

AUSTRALIA

SOUTH AMERICA

ALMOST PATRIMONY
Unlike the rest of the world, almost no placental mammals live in Australia and its neighboring islands. The island continent possesses 83 percent of the unique (endemic) species of mammals.

OPOSSUMS
Family Didelphidae
They spend most of their lives perched in trees and are very timid.

Mammals Colonizing the World

 The first fossils of marsupials and placental mammals were found in rocks dating from the late Jurassic and the earliest part of the Cretaceous periods. At that time, America, Africa, and Australia were united in a single continent (Gondwana) and were beginning to separate. But the placental mammals evolved further, and at the beginning of the Eocene Period (56 million years ago), opossums were the only representatives in America of marsupials, which otherwise prospered only in Australia's particular climate and geographic isolation.

OVER
300
SPECIES EXIST.

TASMANIAN DEVIL
Family Dasyuridae
The largest of the carnivorous marsupials became extinct in Australia 600 years ago, but it survives on the island of Tasmania. It is a predator the size of a small dog.

Order Monotremata

Infraclass Metatheria

Order Dasyuromorphia

Order Didelphimorphia

Order Diprotodontia

Order Microbiotheria

Order Notoryctemorphia

Order Paucituberculata

Order Peramelemorphia

Subclass Prototheria

Infraclass Eutheria

Commonly called placental mammals, they are the typical mammals. They probably began diversifying during the Cretaceous Period (65-150 million years ago) from a different line of the metatherians. They are characterized by the fact that their embryos are implanted in the uterine cavity and develop an outer layer of cells in close union with the maternal body, the placenta. They receive nutrients directly from the placenta during their development until they are born with their vital organs (except for those responsible for reproduction) fully formed.

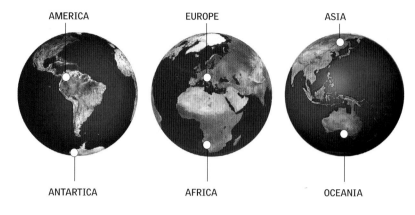

AMERICA   EUROPE   ASIA

ANTARTICA   AFRICA   OCEANIA

THROUGHOUT THE WORLD
The eutherians, or placental mammals, are the most important group of mammals because of the number of living species they represent. Their geographic distribution covers almost the entire planet, including on and beneath bodies of water and polar areas. These animals cover a wide range of ecosystems and forms of life and make up 19 orders of viviparous placental mammals.

Jurassic Beaver

Scientists thought that mammals were able to conquer the Earth only after dinosaurs became extinct. But the recent find of a fossil of this beaver in China suggested that, by the Jurassic Period, when the giant reptiles were at their peak, mammals had already diversified and adapted to water ecosystems 100 million years earlier than had been believed. The *Castorocauda lufrasimilis* lived 140 million years ago.

RACCOON
Order Carnivora
Live in forests near rivers. These carnivorous hunters and climbers live in North America.

Infraclass Eutheria

Order Artiodactyla
Order Carnivora
Order Cetacea
Order Chiroptera
Order Dermoptera
Order Hyracoidea
Order Insectivora
Order Lagomorpha
Order Macroscelidea
Order Perissodactyla
Order Pholidota
Order Primates
Order Proboscidea
Order Rodentia
Order Scandentia
Order Sirenia
Order Tubulidentata
Superorder Xenarthra

Subclass Theria

GIRAFFE
Order Artyodactilae
These are the tallest of living land animals—they can be over 18 feet tall (5.5 m). They are herbivores. Their blood pressure is almost twice that of other large mammals, and their tongues are over 18 inches (0.5 m) long. They live in Africa.

NECK
allows them to reach the highest leaves.

SEALS
Order Carnivora
Along with elephant seals, they make up the Pinnipedia suborder. They move very clumsily on land, but they are very good swimmers. They feed on fish and crustaceans and prefer to inhabit marine waters near the poles, although they reproduce on dry land.

SKIN
A fur coat and subcutaneous fat protect the animal from extreme cold.

THERE ARE OVER
4,000
SPECIES OF EUTHERIANS.

MANDRILL
Order Primates
Weighing up to 120 pounds (55 kg), these are the largest monkeys in the world. The males are much larger than the females, and they have a brilliantly colored face, with deep grooves running down both sides of their snout. Mandrills live in Africa's tropical zones. They are omnivores, eating anything from grasses to small mammals.

What Is a Mammal?

Mammals share a series of characteristics that distinguish their class: a body covered by hair, the birth of live young, and the feeding of newborns on milk produced by the females' mammary glands. All breathe through lungs, and all possess a closed, double circulatory system and the most developed nervous systems in the animal kingdom. The ability to maintain a constant body temperature has allowed them to spread out and conquer every corner of the Earth, from the coldest climates to hot deserts and from the mountains to oceans. ●

A Body for Every Environment

Skin covered with hair and sweat glands helps create and maintain a constant body temperature. At the same time, with eyes placed on each side of the head (monocular vision, with the sole exception of the primates, which have binocular vision), they are afforded important angles of sight. Limbs are either of the foot or chiridium type, with slight variations depending on the part of the foot used for walking. In aquatic mammals, the limbs have evolved into fins; in bats, into wings. Hunters have powerful claws, and unguligrades (such as horses) have strong hooves that support the whole body when running.

BOTTLENOSE DOLPHIN
Tursiops truncatus

Hair

Body hair is unique to mammals and absent in other classes of animals. Sirenians, with little hair, and cetaceans are exceptions; in both cases, the absence of hair is a result of the mammal's adaptation to an aquatic environment.

Dentition

The majority of mammals change dentition in their passage to adulthood. Teeth are specialized for each function: molars for chewing, canines for tearing, and incisors for gnawing. In rodents such as chipmunks, the teeth are renewed by continuous growth.

CHIPMUNK
Family Sciuridae

5,416
THE NUMBER OF MAMMAL SPECIES ESTIMATED TO EXIST ON EARTH

Close Relatives

Humans belong to the primate group. Hominids (orangutans, gorillas, and chimpanzees) are the largest of these, weighing between 105 and 595 pounds (48-270 kg). In general, males are larger than females, with robust bodies and well-developed arms. Their vertical carriage differentiates their skeletons from those of other primates. Gorillas inhabit only the equatorial jungles of western Africa. They support themselves on their forelimbs while walking. Normally their height varies between 4 and 6 feet (1.2-1.8 m), but, if they raise their forelimbs and stand erect, they can be over 6.5 feet tall (2 m).

CRANIUM
Relatively large compared to the size of the body. And the brain is more developed and more complex than that of any other animal.

ALWAYS 98º F (37º C)
The ability to maintain a constant body temperature is not a characteristic unique to mammals; birds also have that ability.

The tiny bones of the ear form a system for sensing and transmitting sound.

Formed by a single bone, called the dentary, and teeth specialized for each function. The entire cranium has a very simplified bone structure.

MAMMARY GLANDS
Secrete the milk with which the females feed their young during their first months of life. These glands give the class its name.

A THICK
Formed by an outer layer (epidermis), another deeper layer (dermis), and a fatty substratum that contributes to homeothermy.

GORILLA
Gorilla gorilla

Homeothermy

The ability to keep body temperature relatively constant, independent of the ambient temperature. Hibernating species are the exception; they must lower their body temperature to enter into this state of reduced metabolic activity. Contrary to popular belief, bears do not truly hibernate but rather enter into a period of deep sleep during winter.

GRIZZLY BEAR (BROWN BEAR)
Ursus arctos

Limbs

Mammals have four limbs that are adapted for moving about on land. Their forelimbs have certain other abilities (swimming, manipulation, attack and defense, protection). The exceptions are the cetaceans, so adapted to marine life that they only have two fingerless limbs, and seals (Phocidae).

ELEPHANT SEALS
Family Phocidae

Take Habitat into Account

Between every mammal and its natural habitat there is a relationship that exists and is expressed in the animal's physical characteristics. Just as the flippers of the elephant seal are used to swim and hunt fish, mimicry and running are vital for deer. Physiology is a special instrument of adaptation to the environment, as in the case of the camel.

Aquatic	Temperate Forests	Desert	Meadow or Pastureland
Tropical Savanna	Tropical Rainforest	Taiga	Tundra

AN UNCOMMON PRIMATE
Humans have adapted to almost all habitats through their ability to modify certain elements of their habitat to their advantage. They often create tools to help them adapt to their environment. In this way, they do not need to rely on natural evolution alone.

Constant Heat

Mammals are homeothermic—which means they are capable of maintaining a stable internal body temperature despite environmental conditions. This ability has allowed them to establish themselves in every region of the planet. Homeostasis is achieved by a series of processes that tend to keep water levels and concentrations of minerals and glucose in the blood in equilibrium as well as prevent an accumulation of waste products—among other things. ●

A Perfect System

➤ Polar bears, like all mammals, keep their internal temperature constant. These bears tolerate the extreme cold of the Arctic ice because they have developed a sophisticated system to increase their ability to isolate and capture sunlight. Their transparent hair receives a large part of it and therefore appears to be white. The hair transmits this light inward, where there is a thick layer of black skin, an efficient solar collector. Their fur is made up of hollow hairs, approximately 6 inches (15 cm) long, which insulate the bear in low temperatures and keep the skin from getting wet when in the water.

Great Swimmers

Polar bears swim with ease in open waters and reach a speed of 6 miles an hour (10 km/h). They propel themselves with their great front paws and use their back feet as rudders. The bear's hair is hollow and filled with air, which helps with buoyancy. When the bear dives, its eyes remain open.

POLAR BEAR
Ursus maritimus

SHELTERED CUBS

The cubs are born in winter, and the skin of the mother generates heat that protects the cubs from the extreme cold.

Migration

WHEN SPRING BEGINS, THESE BEARS TRAVEL SOUTH, ESCAPING THE BREAKUP OF THE ARCTIC ICE.

Metabolism

The layer of fat is between 4 and 6 inches (10-15 cm) thick and provides not only thermal insulation but also an energy reserve. When the temperature reaches critical levels—at the Pole it can drop to between -60° and -75° F (-50° to -60° C)—the animal's metabolism increases and begins to rapidly burn energy from fat and food. In this way, the polar bear maintains its body temperature.

UNDER THE ICE

Females dig a tunnel in the spring; when they become pregnant, they hibernate without eating and can lose 45 percent of their weight.

SECONDARY ACCESS TUNNEL

CHAMBER OR REFUGE

RESPIRATORY PATHWAYS

The bears have membranes in their snouts that warm and humidify the air before it reaches the lungs.

HAIR

An impermeable, translucent surface

Hollow chamber with air

MAIN ACCESS TUNNEL

ENTRANCE

LAYERS

GUARD HAIRS
Outer

UNDERFUR
Inner

FAT
4-6 inches (10-15 cm) thick

Curling Up

Many cold-climate mammals curl up into balls, covering their extremities and bending their tails over their bodies as a kind of blanket. In this way, the surface area subjected to heat loss will be minimal. Hot-climate animals stretch out their bodies to dissipate heat.

PRINCIPAL FAT RESERVES
Thighs, haunches, and abdomen

over
6 miles (10 km)

PER HOUR IS THE AVERAGE SPEED AT WHICH POLAR BEARS SWIM.

SLOW AND STEADY SWIMMING

Hind Legs
function as a rudder.

Forelimbs
function as a motor.

AND FINALLY . . . THE FLOATING SLAB

When they tire of swimming, they rest, floating. They manage to cross distances of over 37 miles (60 km) in this manner.

TO GET OUT: ANTISLIP PALMS

Their palms have surfaces with small papillae that create friction with ice, keeping them from slipping.

HYDRODYNAMIC ANATOMY

What They Are Like

All mammals have stereoscopic vision, which gives them depth perception. Moreover, in the case of hunters such as tigers, their night vision is six times keener than that of humans. There are many species that have a very keen sense of smell, and the sense of taste is closely linked to that of smell. Hair, too, performs

various functions in these animals' lives—conserving body heat, providing protection, and serving as camouflage. Those that have almost no hair and live in environments where the temperature is very low, such as whales, have developed a layer of fat under their skins. ●

Grace and Movement

Horses, one of the odd-toed, hoofed, ungulate mammals, are considered symbols of grace and freedom. They have great vigor and can run swiftly because their spine bends very little, preventing unnecessary expenditure of energy during the rising and falling of their body mass. They are equipped with strong, light, and flexible bones, and their muscles work by contraction, arranged in pairs or groups that pull in opposing directions. ●

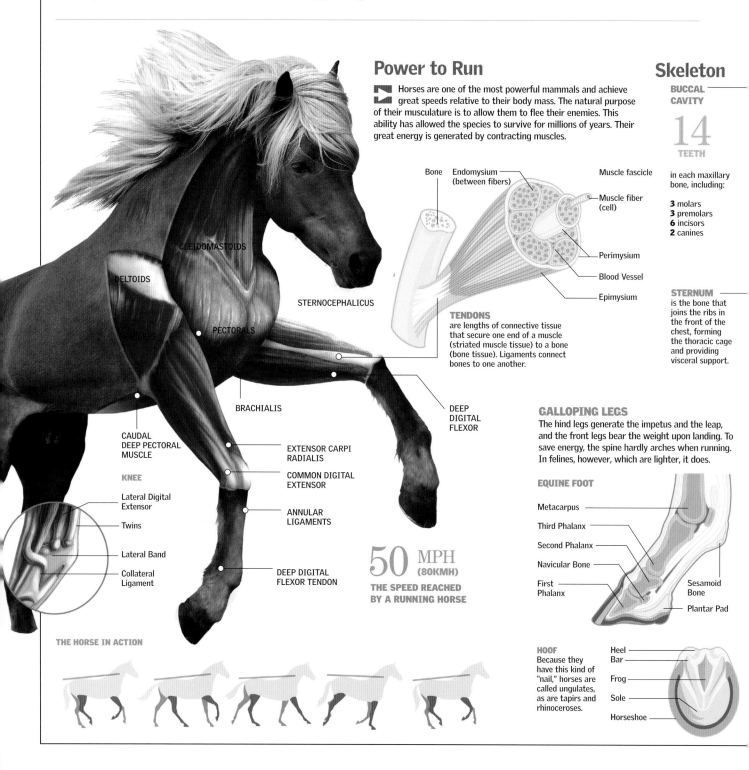

Power to Run

Horses are one of the most powerful mammals and achieve great speeds relative to their body mass. The natural purpose of their musculature is to allow them to flee their enemies. This ability has allowed the species to survive for millions of years. Their great energy is generated by contracting muscles.

Bone
Endomysium (between fibers)
Muscle fascicle
Muscle fiber (cell)
Perimysium
Blood Vessel
Epimysium

TENDONS
are lengths of connective tissue that secure one end of a muscle (striated muscle tissue) to a bone (bone tissue). Ligaments connect bones to one another.

CLEIDOMASTOIDS
DELTOIDS
STERNOCEPHALICUS
PECTORALS
BRACHIALIS
DEEP DIGITAL FLEXOR
CAUDAL DEEP PECTORAL MUSCLE
EXTENSOR CARPI RADIALIS
COMMON DIGITAL EXTENSOR
KNEE
ANNULAR LIGAMENTS
Lateral Digital Extensor
Twins
Lateral Band
Collateral Ligament
DEEP DIGITAL FLEXOR TENDON

50 MPH (80KMH)
THE SPEED REACHED BY A RUNNING HORSE

THE HORSE IN ACTION

Skeleton

BUCCAL CAVITY

14 TEETH

in each maxillary bone, including:

3 molars
3 premolars
6 incisors
2 canines

STERNUM
is the bone that joins the ribs in the front of the chest, forming the thoracic cage and providing visceral support.

GALLOPING LEGS

The hind legs generate the impetus and the leap, and the front legs bear the weight upon landing. To save energy, the spine hardly arches when running. In felines, however, which are lighter, it does.

EQUINE FOOT

Metacarpus
Third Phalanx
Second Phalanx
Navicular Bone
First Phalanx
Sesamoid Bone
Plantar Pad

HOOF
Because they have this kind of "nail," horses are called ungulates, as are tapirs and rhinoceroses.

Heel
Bar
Frog
Sole
Horseshoe

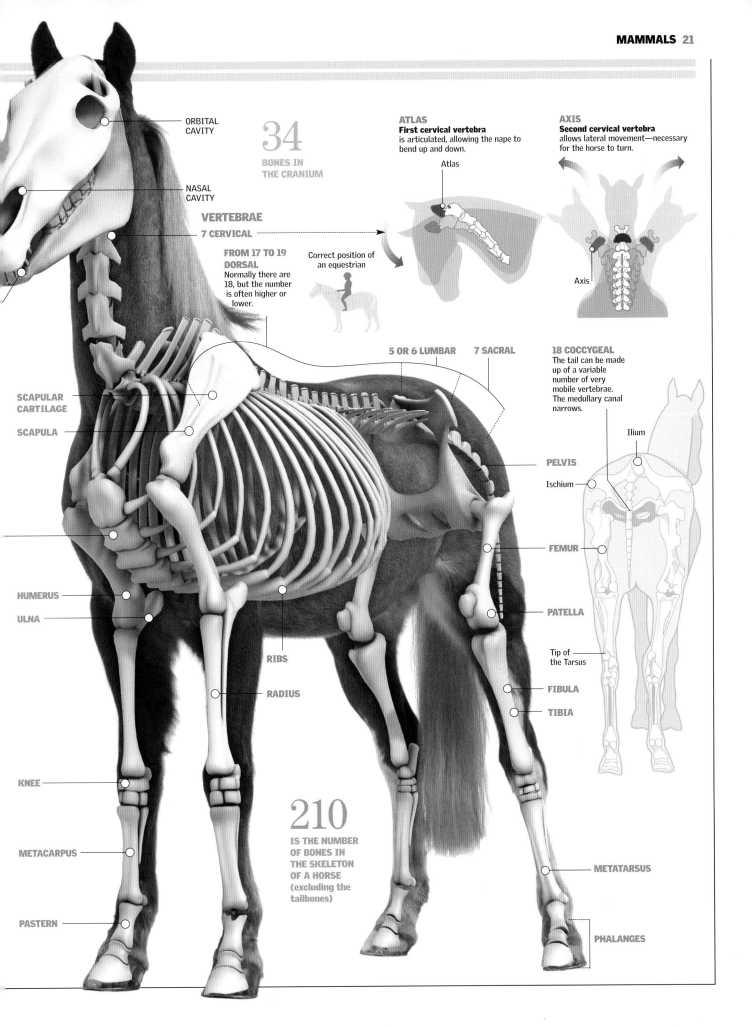

ORBITAL
CAVITY

NASAL
CAVITY

34
BONES IN
THE CRANIUM

VERTEBRAE
7 CERVICAL

**FROM 17 TO 19
DORSAL**
Normally there are
18, but the number
is often higher or
lower.

Correct position of
an equestrian

ATLAS
First cervical vertebra
is articulated, allowing the nape to
bend up and down.

Atlas

AXIS
Second cervical vertebra
allows lateral movement—necessary
for the horse to turn.

Axis

5 OR 6 LUMBAR   **7 SACRAL**

18 COCCYGEAL
The tail can be made
up of a variable
number of very
mobile vertebrae.
The medullary canal
narrows.

Ilium

Ischium

PELVIS

SCAPULAR
CARTILAGE

SCAPULA

FEMUR

PATELLA

HUMERUS

ULNA

Tip of
the Tarsus

RIBS

FIBULA

TIBIA

RADIUS

KNEE

210
IS THE NUMBER
OF BONES IN
THE SKELETON
OF A HORSE
(excluding the
tailbones)

METACARPUS

METATARSUS

PASTERN

PHALANGES

Extremities

M ammals' extremities are basically either of the foot or chiridium type but modified according to the way in which each species moves about. Thus, for example, they become fins for swimming in aquatic mammals and membranous wings in bats. In land mammals, these variations depend on the way the animal bears its weight in walking: those that use the whole foot are called plantigrades; those that place their weight on their digits, digitigrades; and those that only touch the ground with the tips of their phalanges, ungulates.

Functionally Adapted

Another criterion for classifying mammals by their legs, in addition to their morphology, is the function the legs perform. Cats, dogs, and horses have four limbs for locomotion. Primates have differentiated forelimbs, and they also use legs to capture food or bring it to their mouth. Others use legs to swim or fly.

SECOND TOE

LEFT FOOT OF CHIMPANZEE
Pan troglodytes
Life-size photo

NAIL

DISTAL PHALANX

BIG TOE

MEDIAL PHALANX

PHALANX

METATARSAL

KEY
- Tibia/Fibula
- Tarsi
- Metatarsi
- Phalanges

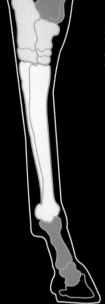

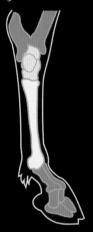

UNGULIGRADE I
HORSES
If you observe their footprints, you will see that only their hooves leave marks. Horses' hooves are made up of only one toe.

UNGULIGRADE II
GOATS
The majority of ungulates, such as goats, have an even number of toes. They are called artiodactyls as opposed to perissodactyls, which have an odd number of toes.

5 toes
THE NORMAL NUMBER FOR MAMMALS: RUNNING SPECIES HAVE FEWER.

WALK OR CLIMB
There is a fundamental difference between the human foot and that of a monkey. The monkey has a long, prehensile digit in its foot similar to that in its hand. Monkeys use their feet to grab branches as they move through the trees.

Chimpanzee   **Human**

Small

LYING FOOTPRINTS
Other species of unguligrades (or simply ungulates) can have more toes that make up their hooves, but they do not place weight on more than two of them.

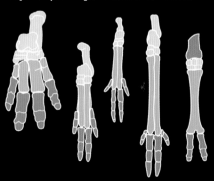

HIPPOPOTAMUS   PIG   CHEVROTAIN   DEER   CAMEL

DIGITIGRADE
DOG
These mammals place the full surface of their toes (or some of them) on the ground when walking. They usually leave the mark of their front toes and a small part of the forefoot as a footprint. Dogs and cats are the best-known examples.

PLANTIGRADE
HUMAN
Primates, and of course humans, bear their weight on their toes and much of the sole of the foot when walking, particularly on the metatarsus. Rats, weasels, bears, rabbits, skunks, raccoons, mice, and hedgehogs are also plantigrades.

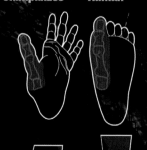

TARSI

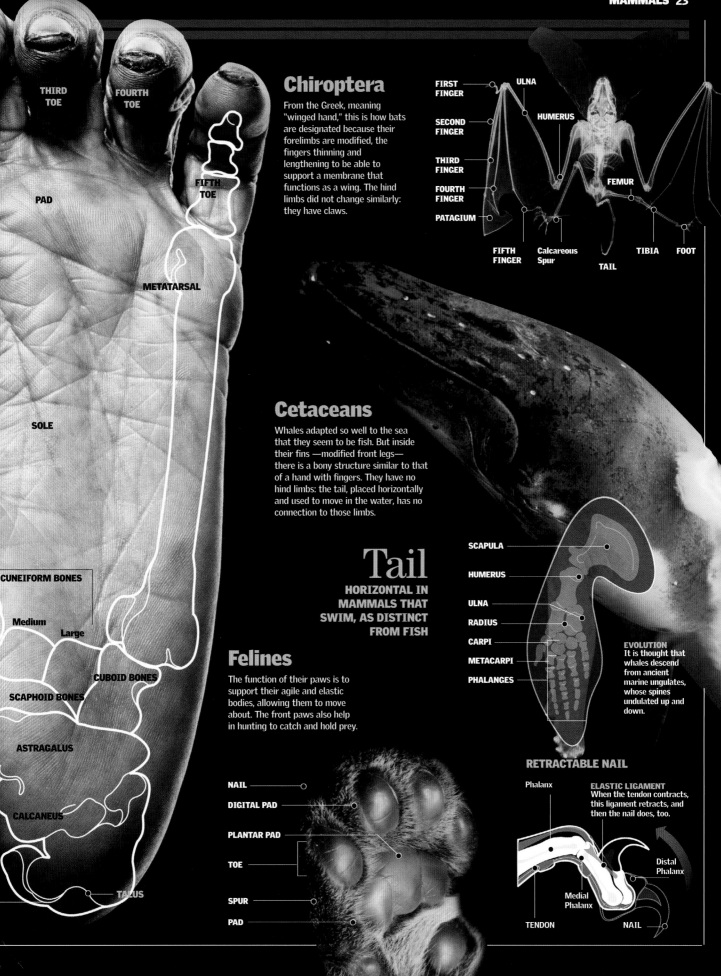

THIRD TOE

FOURTH TOE

FIFTH TOE

PAD

METATARSAL

SOLE

CUNEIFORM BONES

Medium

Large

CUBOID BONES

SCAPHOID BONES

ASTRAGALUS

CALCANEUS

TALUS

Chiroptera

From the Greek, meaning "winged hand," this is how bats are designated because their forelimbs are modified, the fingers thinning and lengthening to be able to support a membrane that functions as a wing. The hind limbs did not change similarly: they have claws.

FIRST FINGER
ULNA
SECOND FINGER
HUMERUS
THIRD FINGER
FOURTH FINGER
FEMUR
PATAGIUM

FIFTH FINGER
Calcareous Spur
TIBIA
FOOT
TAIL

Cetaceans

Whales adapted so well to the sea that they seem to be fish. But inside their fins —modified front legs— there is a bony structure similar to that of a hand with fingers. They have no hind limbs: the tail, placed horizontally and used to move in the water, has no connection to those limbs.

Tail

HORIZONTAL IN MAMMALS THAT SWIM, AS DISTINCT FROM FISH

SCAPULA
HUMERUS
ULNA
RADIUS
CARPI
METACARPI
PHALANGES

EVOLUTION
It is thought that whales descend from ancient marine ungulates, whose spines undulated up and down.

Felines

The function of their paws is to support their agile and elastic bodies, allowing them to move about. The front paws also help in hunting to catch and hold prey.

NAIL
DIGITAL PAD
PLANTAR PAD
TOE
SPUR
PAD

RETRACTABLE NAIL

Phalanx

ELASTIC LIGAMENT
When the tendon contracts, this ligament retracts, and then the nail does, too.

Distal Phalanx

Medial Phalanx

TENDON
NAIL

What Doesn't Run, Flies

They are meteors of flesh, bone, and hot blood. Cheetahs are the fastest of the land animals and unique members of the Felidae family, which hunt using their keen vision and great speed. They can reach over 70 miles per hour (115 km/h) in short runs and reach 45 miles per hour (72 km/h) in an average of only 2 seconds. They can get above 60 miles per hour (100 km/h), but they can sustain that speed for only a few seconds. They look like leopards, although their physical characteristics are different: they are longer and thinner, and their heads are smaller and rounded. ●

TAKEOFF
From the top of a tree, it jumps toward another shorter tree.

Cheetahs

Whereas tigers prefer to lie in wait for prey and then jump on it, the cheetah uses explosive speed of over 60 miles per hour (100 km/h) to run its prey down.

 START
The cheetah begins running by lengthening its stride and extending its four legs.

 SPINAL CONTRACTION
Then it gathers its legs under its body, contracting its cervical spine to the maximum.

NOSTRILS
Very wide, they allow it to receive more oxygen as it runs.

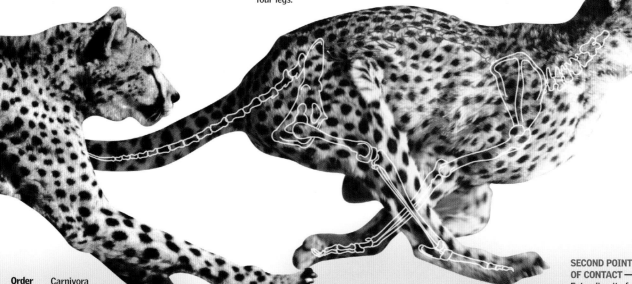

Order	Carnivora
Family	Felidae
Species	*Acinonyx jubatus* (Africa)
	Acinonyx venaticus (Asia)

FIRST POINT OF CONTACT
As it runs, only one leg touches the ground at a time, but during the cervical contraction, the entire body lifts from the ground.

SECOND POINT OF CONTACT
Extending its four legs again, it picks up more momentum, supporting itself only on one back leg.

BIPEDS VERSUS QUADRUPEDS

18 MPH (29 KM/H) SIX-LINED RACERUNNER	23 MPH (37 KM/H) HUMAN BEING	42 MPH (67 KM/H) GREYHOUND	50 MPH (80 KM/H) HORSE	70 MPH (115 KM/H) CHEETAH
Cnemidophorus sexlineatus	Track record: Asafa Powell (Jamaica), 110 yards (100 m) in 9.77 seconds	A dog with a light skeleton and aerodynamic anatomy	An anatomy designed for running, powerful musculature	It only takes 2 seconds to reach a speed of 45 miles per hour (72 km/h).

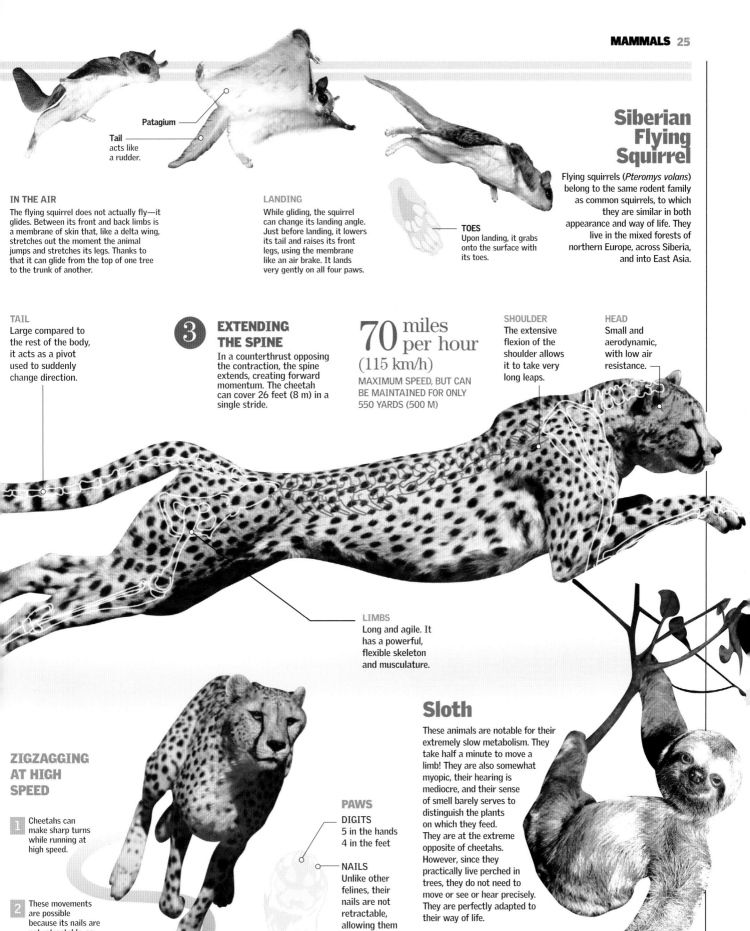

Patagium

Tail
acts like
a rudder.

IN THE AIR
The flying squirrel does not actually fly—it glides. Between its front and back limbs is a membrane of skin that, like a delta wing, stretches out the moment the animal jumps and stretches its legs. Thanks to that it can glide from the top of one tree to the trunk of another.

LANDING
While gliding, the squirrel can change its landing angle. Just before landing, it lowers its tail and raises its front legs, using the membrane like an air brake. It lands very gently on all four paws.

TOES
Upon landing, it grabs onto the surface with its toes.

Siberian Flying Squirrel

Flying squirrels (*Pteromys volans*) belong to the same rodent family as common squirrels, to which they are similar in both appearance and way of life. They live in the mixed forests of northern Europe, across Siberia, and into East Asia.

TAIL
Large compared to the rest of the body, it acts as a pivot used to suddenly change direction.

3 **EXTENDING THE SPINE**
In a counterthrust opposing the contraction, the spine extends, creating forward momentum. The cheetah can cover 26 feet (8 m) in a single stride.

70 miles per hour
(115 km/h)
MAXIMUM SPEED, BUT CAN BE MAINTAINED FOR ONLY 550 YARDS (500 M)

SHOULDER
The extensive flexion of the shoulder allows it to take very long leaps.

HEAD
Small and aerodynamic, with low air resistance.

LIMBS
Long and agile. It has a powerful, flexible skeleton and musculature.

ZIGZAGGING AT HIGH SPEED

1 Cheetahs can make sharp turns while running at high speed.

2 These movements are possible because its nails are not retractable, so that cheetahs firmly grip the ground.

PAWS
DIGITS
5 in the hands
4 in the feet

NAILS
Unlike other felines, their nails are not retractable, allowing them to grip the ground better.

Sloth
These animals are notable for their extremely slow metabolism. They take half a minute to move a limb! They are also somewhat myopic, their hearing is mediocre, and their sense of smell barely serves to distinguish the plants on which they feed. They are at the extreme opposite of cheetahs. However, since they practically live perched in trees, they do not need to move or see or hear precisely. They are perfectly adapted to their way of life.

THREE-TOED SLOTH
Native to the Amazon River basin

Looks That Kill

Tigers are the largest of the world's felines. Predators par excellence, they have physical skills and highly developed senses that they use to hunt for prey. Their daytime vision is as good as that of humans, except for a difficulty in seeing details. However, at night, when tigers usually hunt, their vision is six times keener than that of a human being, because tigers' eyes have larger anterior chambers and lenses and wider pupils. ●

Seeing Even in the Dark

Hunting animals depend on the keenness of their senses to detect their prey. Felines can dilate their pupils up to three times more than humans, and they see best when light is dim and their prey's movements are very subtle. A system of 15 layers of cells forms a sort of mirror (tapetum lucidum) located behind the retina or back of the eye. This mirror amplifies the light that enters and is also the reason that the animal's eyes shine in the dark. At the same time, their eyes are six times more sensitive to light than those of people. Tigers' nocturnal vision also increases because of the great adaptability of their circular pupils when they are completely open.

BINOCULAR VISION

Part of the field of vision of one eye overlaps that of the other eye, which makes three-dimensional vision possible. Hunters' skills depend on binocular vision, because it allows them to judge the distance and size of their prey.

FOCUS 1

FOCUS 2

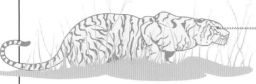

Tigers have a 255° angle of vision, of which 120° is binocular, whereas humans have 210° with 120° of it binocular.

50 times

THE LIGHT AMPLIFICATION CAPABILITY OF THE RETINA OF FELINES

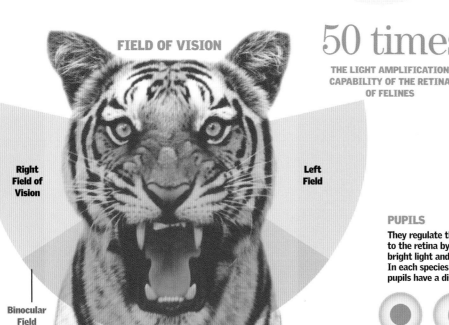

FIELD OF VISION

Right Field of Vision

Left Field

Binocular Field

PUPILS

They regulate the passage of light to the retina by contracting in bright light and dilating in the dark. In each species of mammal, the pupils have a distinctive shape.

TIGER   CAT   GOAT

RETINA

CONJUNCTIVA

CORNEA

LENS

IRIS

PUPIL

VITREOUS HUMOR

OPTIC NERVE

RETINA OF A DIURNAL ANIMAL
Cones, which distinguish colors and details, along with light, predominate.

ROD   CONE

RETINA OF A NOCTURNAL ANIMAL
Rods, super-sensitive to light, predominate.

LIGHTS OR COLORS
The retina's sensitivity to light depends on rod-shaped cells, and forms and colors depend on other cells, which are cone-shaped. In tigers, the former predominate.

Field of Vision

HUMAN

DOG WITH LONG SNOUT

SHORT-SNOUTED DOG

HARE

Developed Senses

Dogs have inherited from wolves great hearing and an excellent sense of smell. Both perform an essential role in their relationship to their surroundings and many of their social activities. However, they are very dependent on the keenness of their senses depending on the habitat in which they develop. Whereas humans often remember other people as images, dogs do so with their sense of smell, their most important sense. They have 44 times more olfactory cells than people do, and they can perceive smells in an area covering some 24 square inches (150 sq cm). Dogs can discern one molecule out of a million other ones, and they can hear sounds so low that they are imperceptible to people. ●

Hearing

The auditory ability of dogs is four times greater than that of human beings, and it is highly developed. Their ability depends on the shape and orientation of their ears, which allow them to locate and pay closer attention to sounds, although this varies by breed. They can hear sharper tones and much softer sounds, and they can directly locate the spatial reference point where a noise was produced. Dogs hear sounds of up to 40 kilohertz, whereas the upper limit for human hearing is 18 kilohertz.

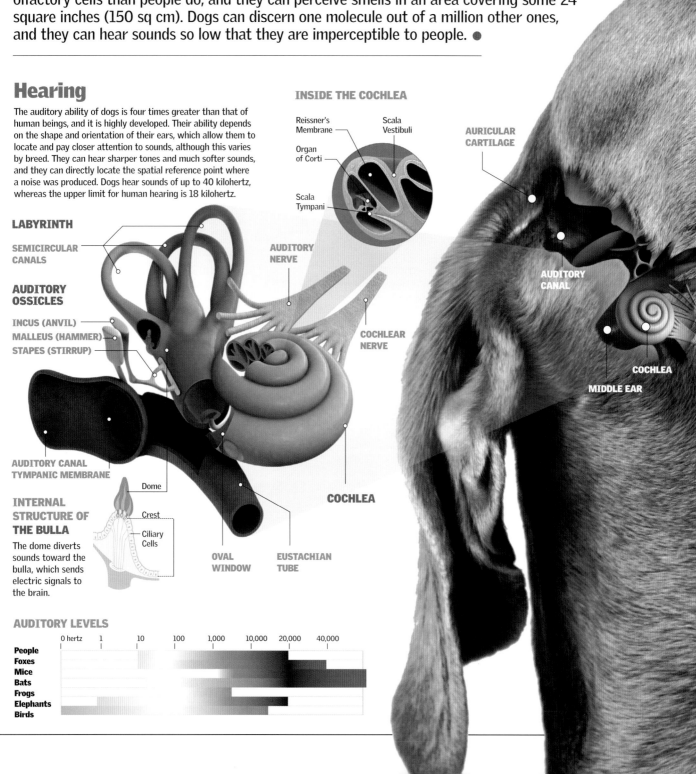

INSIDE THE COCHLEA

Reissner's Membrane
Scala Vestibuli
Organ of Corti
Scala Tympani

AURICULAR CARTILAGE

AUDITORY NERVE

COCHLEAR NERVE

AUDITORY CANAL

COCHLEA

MIDDLE EAR

LABYRINTH

SEMICIRCULAR CANALS

AUDITORY OSSICLES

INCUS (ANVIL)
MALLEUS (HAMMER)
STAPES (STIRRUP)

AUDITORY CANAL
TYMPANIC MEMBRANE

INTERNAL STRUCTURE OF THE BULLA

The dome diverts sounds toward the bulla, which sends electric signals to the brain.

Dome
Crest
Ciliary Cells

COCHLEA

OVAL WINDOW

EUSTACHIAN TUBE

AUDITORY LEVELS

	0 hertz	1	10	100	1,000	10,000	20,000	40,000
People								
Foxes								
Mice								
Bats								
Frogs								
Elephants								
Birds								

TURBINATE BONES

The epithelium that covers these bones is responsible for secreting mucus that traps inhaled particles.

Sense of Smell

Their most developed sense; they have 220 million olfactory cells in their nasal cavities. Mucous tissue, located in the nasal conchae of the snout, warms and moistens the air that they inhale.

Fragrant Material

Dendrites
Mucous Layer

Receptor Cell

Nerve Fiber

over
1,000 times

THE CAPABILITY OF A DOG'S SENSE OF SMELL COMPARED TO THAT OF A HUMAN

Taste

Dogs perceive the chemical substances that foods are made of by means of receptor cells found in the taste buds located at the back of the tongue and in the soft part of the palate.

TASTE BUDS

Dispersed throughout the tongue. Complex interactions among them determine taste by means of nerve endings.

TASTE RECEPTORS

Individual receptor cells pass information to the olfactory centers of the brain.

THE TONGUE AND TASTES

Sweet tastes are experienced in the front part of the tongue, sour ones in the center, and salty ones in the back. On either side salty and sweet are mixed.

SALTY

SOUR

SALTY/SWEET

SALTY/SWEET

SWEET

Behavior and Life Cycle

EAT TO LIVE
An hour after birth, the giraffe gets up and with its 8 feet (2.5 m) of height begins to take its first steps in search of its mother's teat.

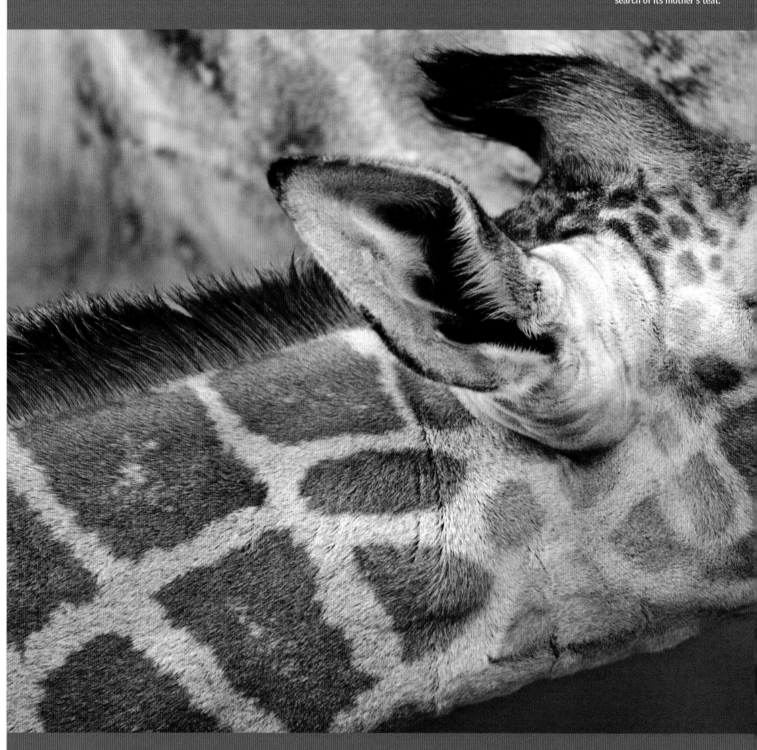

M ammalian reproduction is sexual and by internal fertilization, which involves copulation between the male and the female. Mammals are also characterized by the offspring's dependence on its parents. In any case, there is a group of mammals called monotremes that is oviparous; that is, its members

reproduce by laying eggs. Mammalian behavior consists of a mixture of inherited components and components that can be shaped by learning. Part of this process is accomplished through play, since the young use such encounters to practice jumping, biting, hunting, and other survival skills. You will discover this and much more when you turn the page. ●

Life Cycle

B irth, maturity, reproduction, and death: this life cycle has certain particularities among mammals. As a general rule, the larger a mammal, the longer the members of its species tend to live but the fewer offspring are born to a single female per litter or reproductive season. Most mammals, including humans, are placental mammals; their vital functions are fully developed inside the body of the mother. ●

90 Years
A WHALE'S AVERAGE LIFE SPAN—THE GREATEST OF ANY LIVING MAMMAL

Placental Mammals

This is the largest group of mammals, the one that has multiplied most on the planet, although its form of gestation and lactation produces great wear and tear on the females, making them less prolific. They are generally polygenetic: a few males (the most competitive) fertilize many females, and other males, none. Only 3 percent of mammals are monogamous in each season. In these cases, males participate in rearing the offspring, as they also do when resources are scarce. If resources are abundant, the females take care of the young alone, and the males mate with other females.

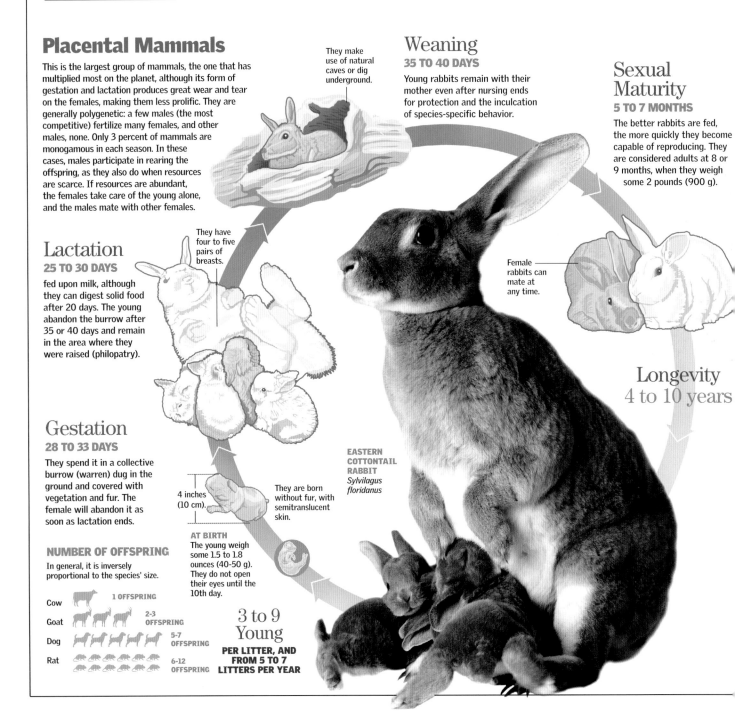

They make use of natural caves or dig underground.

Weaning
35 TO 40 DAYS

Young rabbits remain with their mother even after nursing ends for protection and the inculcation of species-specific behavior.

Sexual Maturity
5 TO 7 MONTHS

The better rabbits are fed, the more quickly they become capable of reproducing. They are considered adults at 8 or 9 months, when they weigh some 2 pounds (900 g).

They have four to five pairs of breasts.

Lactation
25 TO 30 DAYS

fed upon milk, although they can digest solid food after 20 days. The young abandon the burrow after 35 or 40 days and remain in the area where they were raised (philopatry).

Female rabbits can mate at any time.

Longevity
4 to 10 years

Gestation
28 TO 33 DAYS

They spend it in a collective burrow (warren) dug in the ground and covered with vegetation and fur. The female will abandon it as soon as lactation ends.

4 inches (10 cm).

They are born without fur, with semitranslucent skin.

EASTERN COTTONTAIL RABBIT
Sylvilagus floridanus

AT BIRTH
The young weigh some 1.5 to 1.8 ounces (40-50 g). They do not open their eyes until the 10th day.

NUMBER OF OFFSPRING

In general, it is inversely proportional to the species' size.

Cow		1 OFFSPRING
Goat		2-3 OFFSPRING
Dog		5-7 OFFSPRING
Rat		6-12 OFFSPRING

3 to 9 Young
PER LITTER, AND FROM 5 TO 7 LITTERS PER YEAR

Marsupials

Very short gestation period, after which they develop in a sort of partially open pouch (the marsupium), which the female carries on her belly. The majority of the roughly 300 known species of marsupials are solitary, except in mating periods. In general, they are promiscuous animals, although some, such as wallabies (small kangaroos), tend to mate with the same female all their life.

Lactation
22 WEEKS

A muscle inside the pouch prevents the infant from falling out. At 22 weeks, it opens its eyes, and a type of pap produced by its mother is added to its diet, which will prepare it for an herbivorous diet.

Gestation
35 DAYS

With its extremities and functional organs barely developed at birth, the newborn must crawl by itself from the cloaca to the pouch to continue its development.

The young animal fastens itself to its mother and is carried around by her, clinging to her shoulders.

BANISHED OFFSPRING
Dominant males keep the offspring and other young males apart.

Dominant males mate with all the females.

By the end of lactation, fur covers the whole body.

0.8 inch (2 cm)

Some females leave to look for strong males.

KOALA
Phascolarctos cinereus

Leaving the Pouch
1 YEAR

The offspring reaches a size that allows it to fend for itself. It has already incorporated herbivorous food into its diet. The mother can become pregnant again, but its young will remain nearby.

Sexual Maturity
3 TO 4 YEARS

At two years, koalas already have developed sexual organs (females earlier than males). But they do not start mating until one or two years later.

LONGEVITY

People	70 years
Elephants	70
Horses	40
Giraffes	20
Cats	15
Dogs	15
Hamsters	3

Longevity
15 to 20 years

1 offspring
1 BIRTH PER YEAR

GESTATION PERIODS

ANIMAL	MONTHS
Elephants	23
Giraffes	17
Gibbons	9
Lions	7
Dogs	2

COMPARISON OF EGG SIZE

The shell is soft and facilitates the offspring's birth. Unlike birds, they do not have beaks.

Chicken

Echidna

Monotremes

Mammals whose females lay eggs are generally solitary species for most of the year. Platypuses are seen as couples only when they mate. Although they have a period of courtship for one to three months, the males have no relationship with the females after copulation or with the offspring. Short-beaked echidna females practice polyandry, copulating with various males in various seasons.

Incubation
12 DAYS

Eggs gestate for a month before hatching. They incubate within a pouch for about 10 days to remain at the proper temperature until the young are born.

0.5 inch (15 mm)
1 to 3
EGGS AT A TIME

In the Pouch
2 TO 3 MONTHS

After breaking the shell, the young are suckled while they remain in a kind of pouch of the female.

Newborn Offspring

Undeveloped Limbs

Shell

Underground cave or a cave among rocks

The fur is already spiny.

Weaning
4 TO 6 MONTHS

After three months, the offspring can leave the burrow or remain in it alone for up to a day and a half before finally separating from the mother.

Longevity
50 years

SHORT-BEAKED ECHIDNA
Tachyglossus aculeatus

Beauty and Height

Finding a female with whom to mate is the great effort of the male's life, a competition with other males of his own species. Each animal has its particular nuances. For stags, antlers play a fundamental role in winning the heart of their chosen one. Whichever stag has the most beautiful, longest, and sharpest horns will be the winner. Thus, he will be able to defend his territory, court the female, and reproduce.

ANTLER LAYERS

Epidermis
Dermis
Periosteum Fibrous tissue that protects the bone

Red Deer

These are svelte, robust, well-formed animals with a majestic and haughty carriage. They are very timid and fearful, and it is thought that the species is 400,000 years old. They are active at daybreak and evening, and males usually live alone. Females and younger deer group in herds.

Order	Artiodactyla
Family	Cervidae
Species	*Cervus elaphus*
Diet	Herbivorous
Weight (male)	400 pounds (180 kg)

Fights

When two males fight over a harem, each will display his antlers to frighten his rival. The horns can also be used to defend against predators.

24 inches (60 cm)

MALE
43 inches (110 cm)

FEMALE
31 inches (80 cm)

4 NEW

Near the end of summer, stags display their new antlers, which will be larger and heavier than the previous ones.

Horns are shed every year. Animals between the ages of 6 and 10 display the finest antlers.

3

Stags rub their antlers against trees and bushes to get rid of the membrane that covers them.

1

At the onset of autumn, stags begin to lose their antlers, which will be replaced by new ones.

2 GROWTH

New antlers are covered with a fine membrane, called velvet, that will stay on the horns until they are fully developed.

Antlers

FORK   PALM   POINT

BEAM

CROWN

PEDICLE

Horns and Antlers

Horns are outgrowths of the cranium, covered by a tegument that forms a sheath. They appear in bovids of both sexes and are generally permanent. Antlers are also extensions of the cranium; they are limited to the deer family, are present only in males, and are replaced annually.

Bellows

Sonorous and discordant, they begin to be heard when spring arrives, announcing the beginning of rut, or mating season. They not only attempt to keep competitors away with their call but they also use the sound to attract unattached females to join the male's herd.

Oviparous Mammals

For a mammal to lay eggs seems improbable, but the surprising monotreme females, instead of giving birth to young, are oviparous. They are warm-blooded, have hair, and feed their newborn through mammary glands despite having no nipples. Platypuses seem like a cocktail of nature, inasmuch as parts of their bodies resemble those of other types of animal. The other monotremes, echidnas, are covered with spines, and their young grow in the mother's pouch. ●

Platypus

Combining the skin of a mole, the tail of a beaver, the feet of a frog, and the beak of a duck, platypuses are semiaquatic mammals endemic to the eastern part of Australia and to the island of Tasmania. They construct burrows in riverbanks consisting of a long passageway.

Family	Ornithorhynchidae
Species	*Ornithorhynchus anatinus*
Diet	Herbivorous
Weight	5.5 pounds (2.5 kg)

16 TO 24 INCHES (40-60 CM)

BILL
has sensitive electroreceptors that can perceive the electric field generated by the muscles of their prey.

100 feet
(30 m)
HOW LONG THE BURROW OF A PLATYPUS CAN BE

Echidna

Lives in Australia, New Guinea, and Tasmania. It has an elongated snout in the form of a beak, no teeth, and a long, retractable tongue. It is a notable digger and hibernates underground. Echidnas can live up to 50 years, and their hair varies according to the species.

Family	Tachyglossidae
Species	*Tachyglossus aculeatus*
Adult Size	

12 TO 35 INCHES (30 TO 90 CM)

RETRACTABLE TONGUE
A sticky substance on the long and slender tongue allows it to catch termites and ants.

1

Conception

For reproduction, the female
makes a deep burrow, where it
hides. It lays the eggs when it
finishes digging the burrow.

Reproductive Cycle

The platypus has three reproductive cycles annually
and spends most of the year in solitude. Platypuses
are seen as couples only when they mate. They have a
period of courtship before copulation, which is
performed by a juxtaposition of cloacae. Their
reproductive rate is low since they lay only one to
three eggs. The female platypus digs a burrow
before laying her eggs, whereas echidnas have a
pouch in which they incubate their young.
Unlike the hair on the other parts of its
body, the hair in the echidna's
pouch is soft.

2

Incubation

The eggs are covered by
a soft shell, and incubation
lasts two weeks.

3

Birth

When the egg breaks, the
upright position of the
mother allows the offspring
to find the mammary areas.

5

Weaning

After 16 weeks, the young
begin to feed on ants and
other small insects.

4

Lactation

The mother has no nipples,
but milk comes out through
pores in her abdomen, from
which the offspring suck.

EYES
are kept closed
underwater.

SNOUT
is used to
search for and
catch food.

LIMBS
have claws at the tips
of their feet, which help
in digging rapidly.

HAIR
The sharp spines
originate within the fur.

The Cycle

A The egg is the size of a
grape and stays at the
bottom of the female's
incubating pouch. It
takes 11 days to hatch.

1/3 inch
(9 mm)

B When born, it is
one half inch long.
The front feet
hold on to the
mother's pouch,
where it crawls in
search of food.

C Seventy days
later it will leave
the mother's
pouch, and the
mother will place
it in a burrow,
where she will
feed it for three
more months.

Efficient Nursery

M arsupial females carry their newborn offspring in their marsupium, a pouch attached to their belly. The offspring are not very well developed when they come into the world after a gestation period that varies from two to five weeks. Upon emerging, the offspring must immediately climb with their front paws to the marsupium to survive. Once inside, they will be protected. They are continually supplied with milk through their mother's four teats, helping them complete their growth before leaving the pouch for the outside world. ●

Red Kangaroos

Kangaroos are a family comprising several groups, including great wallabies and tree-dwelling kangaroos. Kangaroos, the prototypical marsupial, live in Australia and in Papua New Guinea, never more than 9 miles (15 km) from water. They have large, muscular hind legs that they use to take great consecutive leaps, reaching speeds of 15 to 20 miles per hour (24-32 km/h). They are able to maintain their balance standing only on their hind legs. Their heel bone (calcaneus) is long and acts as a lever.

**4.5 feet
(1.4 m)**

**5 feet
(1.6 m)** **4 feet
(1.3 m)**

Family Macropodidae

Species *Macropus rufus*

Females are half this size.

TEAT
grows in tandem with the offspring and can reach 4 inches (10 cm) long. Then it contracts again.

**TWO
UTERUSES**
The marsupial female has two uteruses.

REPRODUCTIVE CYCLE

0 days BIRTH OF THE KANGAROO		**237 days** A NEW KANGAROO IS BORN	
2 days RUT AND NEW CONCEPTION	**236 days** THE OFFSPRING BECOMES INDEPENDENT	**238 days** RUT AND NEW CONCEPTION	

1 Smoothing the Way

When preparing for the birth of an offspring, the female kangaroo licks its coat to form a kind of path some 5.5 inches (14 cm) long, which the offspring will follow to reach the entrance to the pouch located higher up on the belly.

The female can give birth to an offspring while another one is in the marsupium.

2 A Marathon

Small kangaroos are born after a few weeks of gestation in an early stage of their development, weighing less than 0.2 ounce (5 g). They cannot see or hear. They only move their front paws, with which they drag themselves, following their mother's trail of saliva and guided by their sense of smell.

The baby kangaroo must get to the pouch within three minutes or it will not survive.

**MOVING OUT OF
THE MARSUPIUM**
At eight months, the offspring leaves the pouch and begins to add grass to its diet, but it will continue to be suckled until it is 18 months old.

3 Lactation

Upon reaching the marsupium, the baby fastens its mouth upon one of the four teats inside. At this point, the baby is red and looks very fragile. However, it will grow continuously over the next four months, during which it will not leave the pouch.

Entering the Marsupium

A

After some eight months, the kangaroo can leave the marsupium. But it returns to be suckled and protected.

B

However, it barely fits. It enters head first with the aid of its front paws and turns around once inside the pouch.

C

When it is already alternating milk with grass from outside, the young kangaroo sticks its head out to eat grass without leaving the pouch.

0.8 inch
(20 mm)
THE SIZE OF AN OFFSPRING WHEN IT ENTERS THE MARSUPIUM

Miraculous Placenta

The largest reproductive group is formed by placental mammals, in which the unborn offspring develop in the female's uterus. During gestation, food and oxygen pass from the mother to the fetus through an organ known as the placenta, which allows the exchange of substances through the blood. At birth, the offspring often have no hair, are deaf and blind, and feed on milk secreted by the female's mammary glands, which become active after birth. ●

1 to 2 Days

Rat embryo at the two-cell stage. By the second day, it will have four cells, and on the third day, it will enter the uterus.

2

4 to 5 Days

At this point, the embryo is composed of four cells and is covered with a thin layer of glycoprotein. It implants itself in the uterus.

Gestation of Rats

Gestation lasts between 22 and 24 days. Whereas the placenta is discoid and hemochorial, the ovaries are essential for maintaining gestation. If an ovariectomy is performed at any stage of gestation, it will always bring about a miscarriage or the reabsorption of the fetuses since the placenta does not produce sufficient progesterone to maintain gestation. The growth of the uterine horns becomes visible on the thirteenth day of gestation.

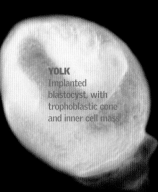

YOLK
Implanted blastocyst, with trophoblastic cone and inner cell mass

3

6 to 8 Days

The blastocyst has now implanted and established itself in the uterus. The fetus begins to form, and the blastocyst becomes a yolk sac.

EYE
begins to develop and can now be observed.

4

11.5 Days

The embryo has now fastened itself to the embryonic sac (a sort of balloon that covers the fetus) and to the placenta. The brain, eyes, and legs begin to form.

BRAIN
The brain is forming; it appears transparent.

ORGANS
Internal organs begin to form and become visible.

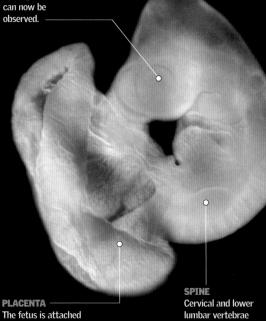

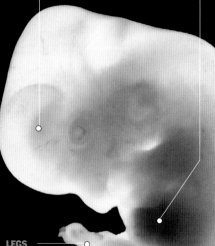

5

14.5 Days

Eyes and extremities are now visible, and the internal organs begin to develop. A pre-cartilaginous maxillary and the outer ear begin to form.

PLACENTA
The fetus is attached to the placenta.

SPINE
Cervical and lower lumbar vertebrae begin to develop.

LEGS
Extremities are in the process of formation.

Placenta

From whales to shrews, placental mammals are characterized by gestating their young inside the mother and giving birth when they are well developed. To do so, they have a special organ, the placenta. This is a spongy tissue that completely surrounds the embryo, allowing the exchange of substances through the blood. In this way, the mother can transfer nutrients and oxygen to the embryo, at the same time that she absorbs the metabolic waste of her future offspring. After birth, the placenta is immediately devoured by the mother, who uses her teeth to help the young leave the structure.

SPINE
The spine can be distinguished and is ready to support the little rat.

EYELIDS
They grow very rapidly, and by day 18 the eyes are already covered.

Uterus
IS BICORNUATE AND HAS TWO CERVICES.

TOES
Toes on the front limbs can also be distinguished.

ORGANS
The organs are now almost complete and ready to go out into the world.

6
17.5 Days
The eyelids grow very rapidly, and within a few hours the eyes will be completely covered. The palate has already completed its development, and the umbilical cord retracts.

7
19.5 Days
Only a few days are left before the female will give birth to a new litter of little rats. At birth, they are helpless despite the fact that all their organs are developed.

0.4 inch (10 mm)

0.6 to 0.8 inch (16 to 20 mm)

The First Days

Mammals whose offspring develop within the uterus devote a lot of attention to their young compared to other animals, because their pups are unable to live on their own at birth. That is why they are cleaned, fed, and warmed. Dogs have various developmental stages. First is the neonatal stage, which lasts from the opening of the pups' eyes until they begin to hear. Then comes the socialization stage, which runs from days 21 to 70, and, finally, the juvenile stage, from 70 days on. ●

Lactation Period

This period is essential in the reproductive process of mammals. The young of most placental mammals are totally dependent in the first stages of their life on mammary milk secretion.

YEARS

4 — **3–4 years**				
3				
2	**18 months**	**18 months**		
1			**7–10 months**	
0				**7 weeks**
Gorilla	Dolphin	Asian elephant	Lion	Dog

Birth

Like humans, dogs develop slowly after birth, because they are not fully developed when they come into this world and are incapable of living on their own. They need a structured environment in which they are cared for by their parents and other members of the pack.

Birth

The first pup is born between 1 and 2 hours after contractions begin.

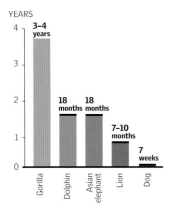

WET HAIR
Once dry, pups seek a teat from which to suck colostrum, which consists of, among other things, immunological substances.

MEMBRANE
Placenta, which covers the pup

Litter
3 to 8 Offspring
The mother knows each newborn and realizes if any pup is taken away from her.

MAMMARY GLANDS

THE DEN
The mother builds a den in a warm place away from noise.

SURPRISE REFLEX
At 20 days, pups start to hear and react to sound.

Up to 20 Days

This period, in which pups depend totally on the mother, lasts from birth to 15 or 20 days, when the pups open their eyes. But until then, they are completely dependent on their mother, seek contact with the mammary glands, and whimper if they are alone. They have little ability to keep themselves warm, and they even need the stimulation of their mother to pass body wastes.

BLIND EYES
Still closed

SKIN
Short and soft hair

The Pups

At birth, pups do not innately recognize members of their species; they do not seem to know that they are dogs. They must learn this, and the mother and the rest of the litter are in charge of teaching them this.

THE MOTHER'S POSITION
The mother lies down to make it easier for the pups to reach her.

TRANSPORT
To move her weak pups, which cannot yet walk, the mother picks them up by the skin on the napes of their necks and places them in the den. Fifteen days after birth, mother dogs experience what is called the bonding phenomenon: they become aware of the litter's existence, see them as a group, and notice if any puppy is missing.

Lost Pup

Den

The mother moves the pups without hurting them.

EYES
remain shut until the second or third week.

THE MOTHER
The relationships of pups to their mother and siblings are essential to dogs' later development, because, although their social structures and relationships are largely innate, they must be shaped, tested, and practiced to develop properly.

STANDING UP
The mother no longer needs to lie down and is free to move away.

TACTILE REFLEX
They push with their snout until they are hidden.

From Day 21 to Day 70

Natural weaning involves offering pups predigested food as a replacement for milk. When the mother comes back from hunting, its mouth has an odor, and the pups, stimulated by the odor, smell her, lick her snout, rub it, and nibble her jaws and face, which stimulates the regurgitation of food. At this stage, in which the pups have milk teeth, they can begin to eat these foods.

EXTENSOR REFLEX
At 12 days, pups extend their hind legs when picked up.

STRENGTH
The pups are now able to be on their own.

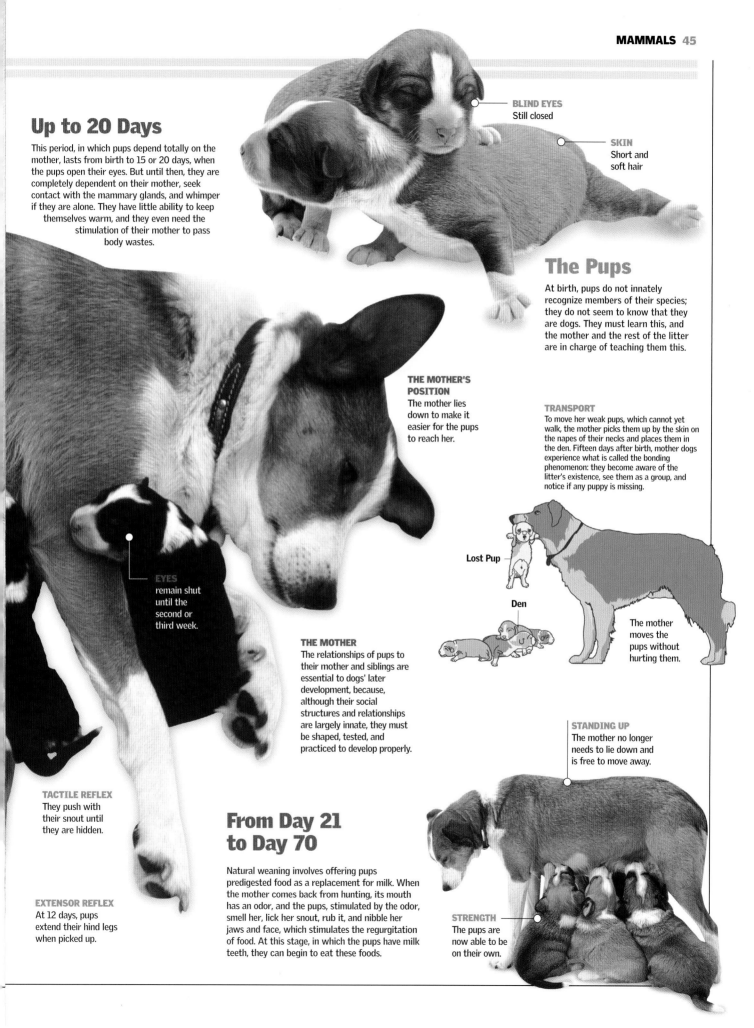

Development and Growth

P lay is much more than entertainment for young mammals. This activity, which may appear to have no specific purpose, is the way in which they learn to be part of their species in the early stages of their lives, simultaneously acquiring the basic means of survival. In their games, chimpanzees perform primary instinctive activities that, with time and improvement, will become perfected instinctive activities. These include using tools, balancing in trees, and forming communication. Young chimpanzees express themselves by means of sounds, facial gestures, and body postures they imitate from adults. Play also allows them to develop their muscle strength and achieve good motor coordination. ●

over 15 TYPES OF CALLS

are emitted by chimpanzees, including its pant-hoot: screams and grunts that can be heard a mile and a quarter (2 km) away. Pant-hoots are unique to the individual and can help to identify each member of the group.

This expression communicates terror.

This expression transmits submission.

This gesture indicates worry.

Communication

Some mammals, especially chimpanzees, communicate through facial expressions. This ability is well developed in the young primates, which express fear, submission, and worry, among other feelings.

Games

What we humans call play appears to be limited only to mammals, because they have well-developed senses, intelligence, and the ability to learn. It is through play that mammals carry out their learning.

Social Relations

Play also helps encourage apes to identify with their species. It provides a basis for learning to communicate through the use of sounds and body posture to express, for example, submission or domination.

IDENTIFICATION
Only 15 minutes of play with peers per day will moderate the effects of social isolation.

Survival

Play also functions as a method of learning to survive in a wild habitat. It trains carnivores in hunting techniques and herbivores in detecting, and fleeing from, danger.

Extremities

Chimpanzees are characterized by their long arms, which are endowed with great strength, and by their opposable thumbs. The digits of their hands and feet are large, allowing them to climb with great ease. They can hold onto a branch with their foot while they pluck its fruit with their hand.

Opposable Thumb

Long Digits

When they move around on all fours, they bear their weight on the soles of the feet and the knuckles of their hands.

Use of Tools

The use of tools is not common in mammals. However, chimpanzees are capable of using objects as tools, a skill they acquire by observing adults. They can use sticks to eat termites or use leaves as spoons to drink water.

words

THEY CAN LEARN AND EXPRESS WORDS USING SIGN LANGUAGE.

PERCEPTION

They have sensory abilities very similar to those of people, and they distinguish smells better. Because of their large brains, they are very intelligent and can communicate with people by signs.

A chimpanzee pokes a stump in search of termites, using a stick as a tool.

A LIFE OF HANGING

A great entertainment for apes is hanging from trees. This exercise improves their coordination and arm strength.

Of Flesh Thou Art

The carnivore group is composed of species whose diet is based on hunting other animals. The kind of teeth they have help them efficiently cut and tear the flesh of their captured prey. Lions, the most sociable of the felines, have good vision and sharp hearing; they live in packs, and when they go hunting, they do so as a group. ●

Lions

are characterized by a strong, muscular physique. A male requires 15.5 pounds of meat (7 kg) a day, whereas a female needs 11 pounds (5 kg). They have a short digestive tract, which rapidly absorbs nutrients from the ingested meat.

Teeth

UPPER PREMOLARS

UPPER CANINE

UPPER INCISORS

CARNASSIAL MOLAR
They are very large, and the dental crowns are two long blades arranged as shears that fit into each other. Together they slice and cut flesh to perfection.

ANTERIOR PREMOLARS

LOWER CANINE

LOWER INCISORS

The Hunt

1 LYING IN AMBUSH
Hidden in the grass, the lioness silently approaches the prey. Other females wait in hiding.

Family	Felidae
Species	*Panthera leo*
Weight	265-410 pounds (120-185 kg)

Size (female)

9 feet (2.7 m)

3 feet (1 m)

SIGHT
Their vision is six times better than that of humans. They also have binocular vision, essential for locating prey.

COAT
Short, with a uniform brown color. They have an off-white tuft of hair on the chin.

Main Prey

The bulk of their diet consists of large mammals, although they also catch small mammals, birds, or reptiles when the opportunity arises. They are not scavengers. They generally eat only fresh meat, something they have killed or succeeded in taking away from another predator.

BUFFALO **ZEBRA** **GIRAFFE**

GNU **GAZELLE** **ANTELOPE**

THE TAIL
Measures some 35 inches (90 cm) in length and allows them to keep their balance while running. They also use it to shoo away flies.

40 pounds (18 kg)
OF MEAT CAN BE EATEN BY A LION IN A SINGLE MEAL.

2 ACCELERATION
When only a few yards away, it starts running to catch the zebra. It exceeds 30 miles per hour (50 km/h), and the other lionesses cooperate in the hunt.

3 LEAP
The lioness hurls the weight of her body on the zebra's neck, trying to knock it down; if she succeeds, the hunt will be successful.

4 LETHAL BITE
The prey falls, and the lioness sinks her fangs into the neck until she kills it. The other females approach.

Herbivores

Ruminants, such as cows, sheep, or deer, have stomachs made of four chambers with which they carry out a unique kind of digestion. Because these animals need to eat large quantities of grass in very short times—or else be easy targets for predators!—they have developed a digestive system that allows them to swallow food, store it, and then return it to the mouth to chew calmly. When animals carry out this activity, they are said to ruminate. •

KEY

▬ INGESTION AND FERMENTATION

▬ RUMINATION

▬ REABSORPTION OF NUTRIENTS

▬ ACID DIGESTION

▬ DIGESTION AND ABSORPTION

▬ FERMENTATION AND DIGESTION

Teeth

Herbivorous animals such as horses and bovids have molars with a large flat surface that reduces food to pulp, as well as incisors for cutting grass. Grinding is also done by the molars.

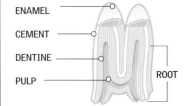

ENAMEL

CEMENT

DENTINE

PULP

ROOT

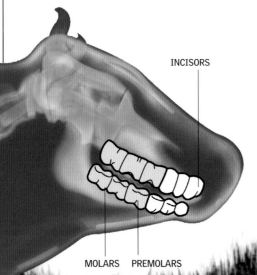

INCISORS

MOLARS   PREMOLARS

Cows wrap their tongues around the food.

Then they chew it with lateral movements.

1

Cows lightly chew grass and ingest it into their first two stomachs: the rumen and the reticulum. Food passes continually from the rumen to the reticulum (nearly once every minute). There various bacteria colonies begin fermenting the food.

RETICULUM

2

When cows feel satiated, they regurgitate balls of food from the rumen and chew them again in the mouth. This is called rumination; it stimulates salivation, and, as digestion is a very slow process, cows make use of rumination to improve their own digestion together with the intervention of anaerobic microorganisms such as protozoa, bacteria, and fungi.

40 gallons (150 l)

OF SALIVA ARE PRODUCED DAILY IN THE PROCESS.

THE RUMINATION PROCESS

helps ruminants reduce the size of the ingested food particles. It is part of the process that allows them to obtain energy from plant cell walls, also called fiber.

Ⓐ REGURGITATION   Ⓑ REMASTICATION   Ⓒ REINSALIVATION   Ⓓ REINGESTION

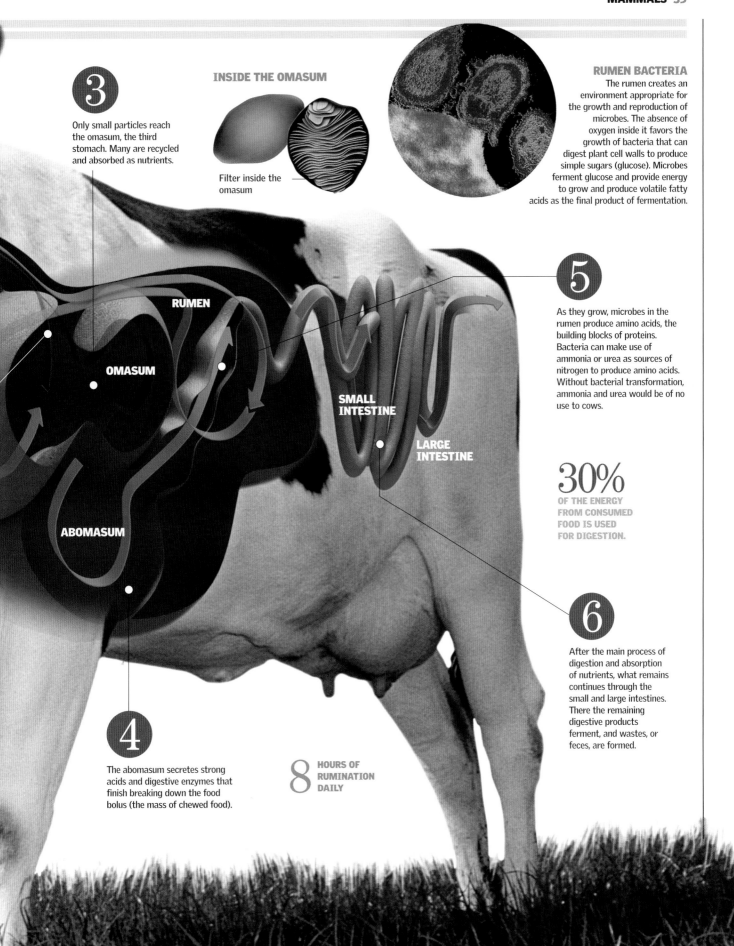

3

Only small particles reach the omasum, the third stomach. Many are recycled and absorbed as nutrients.

INSIDE THE OMASUM

Filter inside the omasum

RUMEN BACTERIA

The rumen creates an environment appropriate for the growth and reproduction of microbes. The absence of oxygen inside it favors the growth of bacteria that can digest plant cell walls to produce simple sugars (glucose). Microbes ferment glucose and provide energy to grow and produce volatile fatty acids as the final product of fermentation.

RUMEN

OMASUM

ABOMASUM

SMALL INTESTINE

LARGE INTESTINE

5

As they grow, microbes in the rumen produce amino acids, the building blocks of proteins. Bacteria can make use of ammonia or urea as sources of nitrogen to produce amino acids. Without bacterial transformation, ammonia and urea would be of no use to cows.

30%
OF THE ENERGY FROM CONSUMED FOOD IS USED FOR DIGESTION.

6

After the main process of digestion and absorption of nutrients, what remains continues through the small and large intestines. There the remaining digestive products ferment, and wastes, or feces, are formed.

4

The abomasum secretes strong acids and digestive enzymes that finish breaking down the food bolus (the mass of chewed food).

8 HOURS OF RUMINATION DAILY

The Great Chain

Maintaining ecological balance requires the existence of prey and predators. Predatorial species bring about a sustained reduction in the number of individuals of the prey species. If predators did not exist, their prey would probably proliferate until the ecosystem collapsed, because there would not be enough food for them all. Disappearance of predators is the cause of many imbalances created in certain habitats by people, whose predatory ability exceeds that of any other living species. Like all other animal species, mammals do not make up a food chain in themselves, instead depending at all times on the participation of plants and other animals. ●

Level 4

Large carnivores are at the top of the food chain—there are no other predatory species that regulate their population.

SMALL-SPOTTED GENET
Like many highly predatory large felines and dogs, it is in danger of extinction as a result of human activity.

Equilibrium of the System

There is a very efficient natural equilibrium in the food chains of a terrestrial ecosystem, of which mammals form various parts. For this balance to be maintained, there can never be more herbivores than plant food or enough carnivores to overwhelm the herbivores. If there were more herbivores than plant food, they would eat all the vegetation and then suffer a drastic population reduction. A similar situation would occur if there were enough carnivores to overwhelm the herbivores.

Level 3

Small carnivores feed on small, herbivorous mammals or on birds, fish, or invertebrates. At the same time, they must be on guard against other, larger species.

Trophic Pyramid

Energy is transferred from one level to another in an ecosystem. At each level, a small amount of energy is lost. What is retained at one level is the potential energy that will be used by the next. Biomass is the total mass of living matter; it can apply to a specific level of the trophic pyramid, a population of individuals of the same species, or a community of different species.

Tertiary Consumers
Secondary Consumers
Primary Consumers
Primary Producers—Plants
Energy Consumed

Competition

Within the same level, different herbivorous rodents (such as rats and prairie dogs) compete with each other for food.

Level 2

Primary consumers devour autotrophic organisms (plants or algae), because they depend on them for subsistence. And other mammals feed on them.

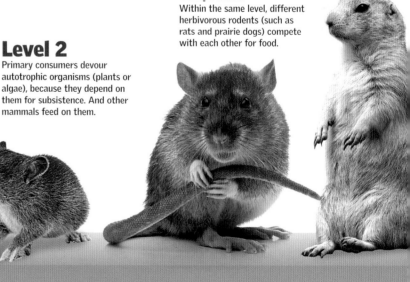

Population

IS GREATER AS ONE GOES DOWN THE PYRAMID.

Level 1

Because of photosynthesis, only plants and algae can transform inorganic matter into organic matter. They form the beginning of the food chain.

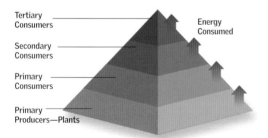

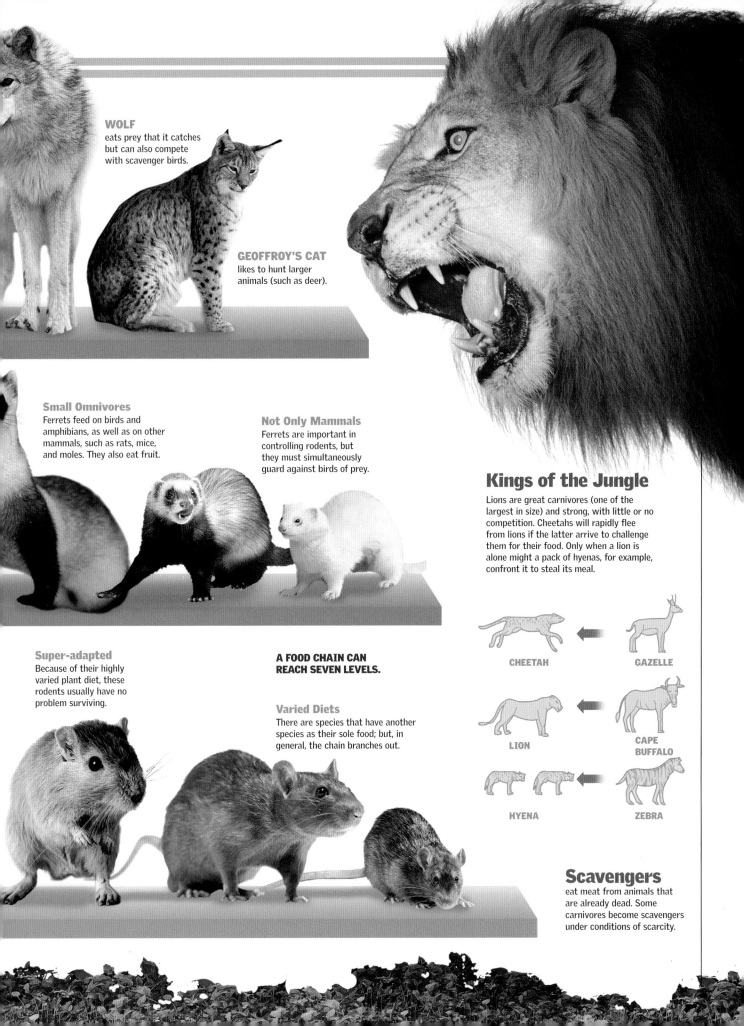

WOLF
eats prey that it catches but can also compete with scavenger birds.

GEOFFROY'S CAT
likes to hunt larger animals (such as deer).

Small Omnivores
Ferrets feed on birds and amphibians, as well as on other mammals, such as rats, mice, and moles. They also eat fruit.

Not Only Mammals
Ferrets are important in controlling rodents, but they must simultaneously guard against birds of prey.

Super-adapted
Because of their highly varied plant diet, these rodents usually have no problem surviving.

A FOOD CHAIN CAN REACH SEVEN LEVELS.

Varied Diets
There are species that have another species as their sole food; but, in general, the chain branches out.

Kings of the Jungle
Lions are great carnivores (one of the largest in size) and strong, with little or no competition. Cheetahs will rapidly flee from lions if the latter arrive to challenge them for their food. Only when a lion is alone might a pack of hyenas, for example, confront it to steal its meal.

CHEETAH ← GAZELLE

LION ← CAPE BUFFALO

HYENA ← ZEBRA

Scavengers
eat meat from animals that are already dead. Some carnivores become scavengers under conditions of scarcity.

One for All

eerkats are small mammals that live in underground colonies, posting guards while the mothers take care of their young. During the day they go above ground to feed, and at night they go into the burrow to take refuge from the cold. In this large family, made up of dozens of members, each one fulfills a function. When faced with danger, they employ various tactics to defend themselves. One of these is the squeal that lookouts emit in the face of even slight dangers.

MEERKAT
Suricata suricatta

Family	Herpestidae
Habitat	Africa
Offspring	2 to 7

12 inches (30 cm)

Weight 2 pounds (1 kg)

ABOUT
30
IS THE NUMBER OF INDIVIDUALS A GROUP CAN HAVE.

Social Structure

➤ The social structure is extensive and well defined, ensuring that everyone has a role to fulfill. The lookouts (which may be female or male) take turns to sound the alarm over the arrival of strangers; one that is better fed replaces another that needs to eat. These animals are carnivorous. They eat small mammals, as well as insects and spiders.

FEMALES
must dedicate all their energy to the process of reproducing and feeding and raising young.

OFFSPRING
When the father or mother standing watch gives the cry of danger, all run to hide in the burrow.

BLACK-BACKED JACKAL
The meerkats' largest predator. To detect one before it is seen is of prime importance for the colony.

MARTIAL EAGLES
The most dangerous enemy they have and the one that kills the greatest number of meerkats

Lookout

When a predator is detected, the lookout warns its group so that all of them can take cover in a nearby hole. This role rotates among different members of the group, and the warning is given by a very wide repertoire of sounds, each of which has a distinct meaning.

MEERKATS ALSO USE VOCALIZATIONS TO COMMUNICATE.

Defense

1

SURROUNDING THE ENEMY
They emit a type of squeal. They rock back and forth. They try to appear larger and more ferocious than they are.

2

ON THEIR BACKS
If this tactic fails, they throw themselves down on their backs to protect their necks, showing their fangs and claws.

3

PROTECTION
When it is an aerial predator, they run to hide. If taken by surprise, adults protect the young.

SIGHT
Binocular and in color, it allows them to locate their greatest predators, birds of prey.

VIGILANCE FROM ABOVE
It is common to see them in the highest places of their territory on **rocks or tree branches.**

is kept permanently erect, observing the burrow's surroundings.

FRONT PAWS
They have strong claws, which they use for digging or to defend themselves.

MALES
defend their territory and stand watch. The dominant male is the reproducer.

Territory

The area defended provides the food necessary for the group's subsistence. Males devote themselves to defense, and when resources run out the group migrates to another area.

BURROWS
They dig them with their sharp claws and leave them only during the day.

HIND FEET
They support themselves on their hind feet when they remain standing, keeping watch.

TRIPOD TAIL
Meerkats use it to balance themselves when they are in an upright position.

Wolves in Society

S ocial units and mutual aid are common in mammals' lives, except for a few species that live alone or in small families. Wolves are social animals that live closely attached to a group—the pack—that forms the basis of their social structure. Behavior in a pack is highly regulated and hierarchical. ●

VOCAL COMMUNICATION plays an important role, allowing wolves to locate pack members.

Hierarchy

There are two hierarchies in the pack: one of males and another of females. At the top of each are the alpha (or dominant) male and female. Underneath this pair is a group of subdominant wolves among whom there may be little or no difference in rank. Among females, a strong dominant-submissive relationship is observed between beta and gamma wolves, as well as of the alpha female over those two.

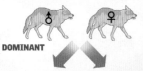

DOMINANT

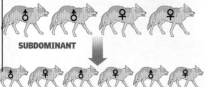

SUBDOMINANT

OFFSPRING

TERRITORY

The highest-ranking adults live in the central area or home. The territory proper lies in the periphery and is inhabited by subadults and members of lower social rank. Between these two areas is that of vital domain, an intermediate area inhabited by all members. The territory can extend over 100 square miles (300 square km).

CENTRAL AREA is inhabited by the highest-ranking animals.

INTERMEDIATE REGION is inhabited indiscriminately by all the wolves.

PERIPHERY, OR TERRITORY is inhabited by wolves of lower social rank.

DOMINATORS

Made up of the breeding pair, which is dominant, and their descendants. Only the breeding pair, however, are permanently dominant. A relationship of dominance-submission between sexes is also established. The alpha female exercises clear dominance over the subdominant males.

DOMINANT PAIR

Recognition of Position

Fights and confrontations within the pack are rituals by means of which relations of power and hierarchical status are established and delimited.

High-ranking   Low-ranking

1 Encounter

The low-ranking wolf advances with submissive posture: ears laid back and its tail between its legs.

GAMES
Although it looks like the wolves are playing in this picture, they are actually carrying out a game involving power and hierarchy.

6 to 20
individuals
IS THE SIZE OF THE PACK DEPENDING ON THE AVAILABILITY OF FOOD.

LEGS IN THE AIR
This posture implies submission and nonaggression.

The Family
Wolves live in packs made up of two to three pairs of adults and their various generations of offspring. They cooperate in hunting, killing animals several times larger than themselves. Although they share food, wolves have a hierarchical order that obliges the young to make way for larger and older family members.

② Examination
It crouches in front of the snout of the dominant and gives it rapid licks, submitting to the hierarchy.

③ Recognition
Then it lies down and urinates while the dominant smells its genitals to identify it.

Diversity

DISTINCTIVE STRIPES
Zebras' stripes extend
down to the underbelly.
They confuse predators.

There is great variety among mammals, and in this chapter we try to show you some representatives of the most outstanding differences among them. For example, here you will discover that there are species, such as bats, that are expert fliers, while others, such as dormice, enter into a deep winter sleep that allows them to save

energy during times when food is scarce. Here we will also show you how the bodies of some mammals (whales and dolphins) are adapted to aquatic life. In addition, we will also consider the ability of certain mammals to adapt to the hot and dry conditions of the desert. Camels, in particular, are very adept when it comes to retaining and efficiently using liquids. ●

Deep Sleep

How many times have you heard the expression "dead as a dormouse"? The comparison is no accident, although it should be understood that dormice do not die: they merely hibernate. In the cold season, low temperatures and scarcity of food lead many mammals to enter into lethargic states. Body temperatures drop, heart rates and respiration slow down, and they lose consciousness. ●

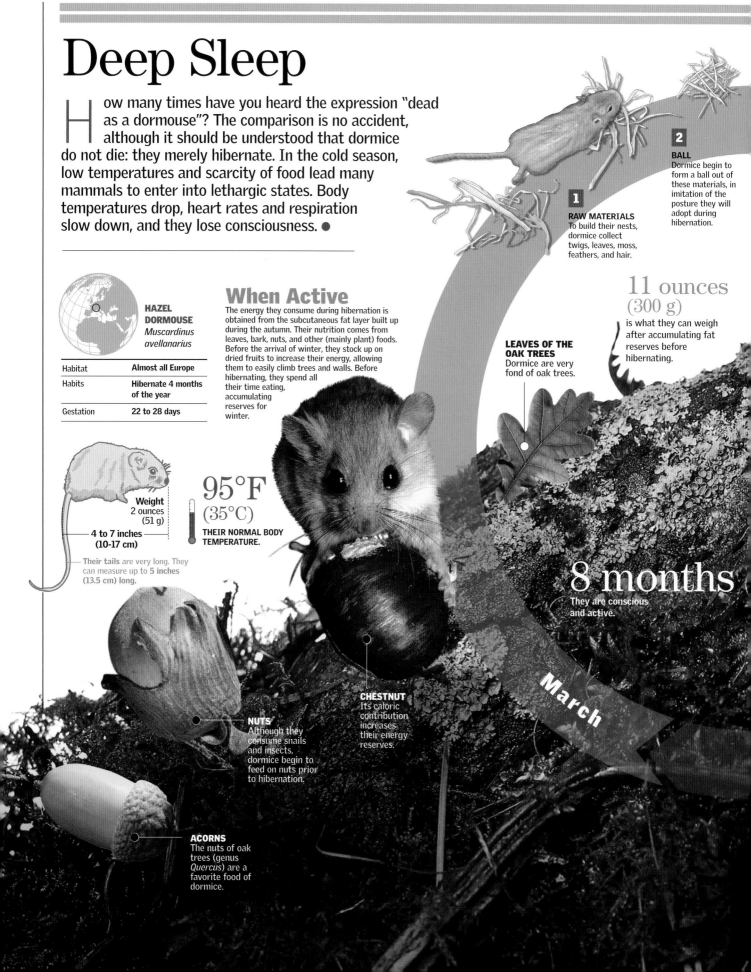

1
RAW MATERIALS
To build their nests, dormice collect twigs, leaves, moss, feathers, and hair.

2
BALL
Dormice begin to form a ball out of these materials, in imitation of the posture they will adopt during hibernation.

HAZEL DORMOUSE
Muscardinus avellanarius

Habitat	Almost all Europe
Habits	Hibernate 4 months of the year
Gestation	22 to 28 days

When Active

The energy they consume during hibernation is obtained from the subcutaneous fat layer built up during the autumn. Their nutrition comes from leaves, bark, nuts, and other (mainly plant) foods. Before the arrival of winter, they stock up on dried fruits to increase their energy, allowing them to easily climb trees and walls. Before hibernating, they spend all their time eating, accumulating reserves for winter.

11 ounces (300 g)
is what they can weigh after accumulating fat reserves before hibernating.

LEAVES OF THE OAK TREES
Dormice are very fond of oak trees.

Weight
2 ounces (51 g)

4 to 7 inches (10-17 cm)

Their tails are very long. They can measure up to 5 inches (13.5 cm) long.

95°F (35°C)
THEIR NORMAL BODY TEMPERATURE.

8 months
They are conscious and active.

March

CHESTNUT
Its caloric contribution increases their energy reserves.

NUTS
Although they consume snails and insects, dormice begin to feed on nuts prior to hibernation.

ACORNS
The nuts of oak trees (genus *Quercus*) are a favorite food of dormice.

Building the Nest

Dormice build their nests out of twigs, moss, and leaves, although they can also hibernate in trees, stone walls, or old buildings, creating a nest from fur, feathers, and leaves. They then settle into the nest, forming a ball. When they cannot find a natural refuge, dormice may settle into birds' nests with total impunity.

3

HOLLOW BALL
Like an ovenbird nest, the ball must be hollow so it can shelter the dormouse.

4

FINISHED NEST
With an entrance in front, the hollow ball has been transformed into a nest.

November

December

February

4 months
They remain in a state of hibernation.

50%
Weight loss after consuming all their reserves

Hibernation

During this period, dormice enter into a deep sleep. Body temperature drops to 34° F (1° C), appreciably decreasing the heart rate. In fact, up to 50 minutes can transpire between breaths. Throughout these months, they slowly use up their reserves, losing up to 50 percent of their body weight. Their endocrine system is almost totally at rest: the thyroid ceases functioning, as does the interstitial tissue of the testicles.

**34°F
(1°C)**
THEIR BODY TEMPERATURE DURING HIBERNATION

POSITION OF THE BODY

TAIL
They cover part of the body with it.

HEAD
They hide it behind their long tail.

FEET
remain flexed during these months.

RESPIRATION
Fifty minutes can pass between breaths.

ENERGY
They obtain it from the subcutaneous fat reserves they accumulated in the fall.

HEART
Heartbeats decrease considerably.

OTHER PLACES FOR HIBERNATION

BIRD'S NEST
If they do not find a place to build their nest, they may take over a bird's nest.

HOLE IN A TREE
can also serve as a burrow for hibernation.

BIORHYTHM OF A DORMOUSE WHILE HIBERNATING

TEMPERATURE

WEIGHT

RESPIRATION

| Prior Feeding | Deep Hibernation | Brief Activity | Deep Hibernation | After Hibernation |

Rationed Water

Camels have developed a sophisticated physiology in order to face life in hot climates. Their kidneys are capable of greatly distilling their urine to prevent water loss. When sandstorms worsen, camels curl up on the ground and close their eyes and nasal openings to protect themselves. When water and food are scarce, they are able to endure by consuming the reserves they have accumulated and stored in the hump and internal sacs. They also have oval-shaped red blood cells, which can easily move throughout the body even when the blood has become thickened from dehydration. ●

DROMEDARY, OR ARABIAN, CAMEL
Camelus dromedarius

Habitat	**Arabia and Africa**
Food	**Herbivorous**
Average life span	**50 years**

Weight
1,300 pounds
(600 kg)

—— 10 feet ——
(3 m)

Characteristics

BODY TEMPERATURE
During the day, their bodies act as heat retainers, and during the night, the excess temperature dissipates by conduction.

NOSE
Their mucus structure is 100 times more complex than that of humans and retains 66 percent of the air's moisture.

HAIR
is so thick that it prevents heat from reaching the skin. When cold is intense, the hair keeps the camel warm with its own body heat.

Kidneys

greatly distill the urine, preventing unnecessary water loss. The urine may get as thick as syrup and contain double the salt of seawater. In this way, camels eliminate impurities and filter the blood, losing as little water as possible.

ERYTHROCYTES

Normal Erythrocyte

Swollen Erythrocyte

240%

The percentage by which an erythrocyte can swell, increasing its ability to transport water.

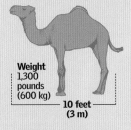

LOOP OF HENLE
recovers part of the water. Because the loop is longer in dromedaries than in any other mammal, water circulates for a very long time.

KIDNEYS
concentrate urine to retain water.

KNEES
have calluses so camels can kneel without getting burned.

The Hump as a Reserve

Formed by the accumulation of fat during periods of abundant food, the hump is an energy reserve that dromedaries use in the absence of plant foods. This chemical reaction provides camels with a small but invaluable amount of metabolic water. The breakdown of the fat produces hydrogen, which combines with inhaled oxygen to produce water. By combining metabolic and cellular water, interstitial lymph, and plasma, they can go without food and water for long periods of time.

34 gallons
(130 l)

THE AMOUNT OF WATER DROMEDARIES CAN CONSUME IN 10 MINUTES

HUMP
Fat accumulates and prevents the excretion of water from the whole body. This allows camels to use a minimum of water.

31 pounds
(14 kg)

HUMPS CAN WEIGH THIS MUCH.

2 pounds = 2 quarts
(1 kg)   (2 l)
of consumed fat   of metabolic water

RESISTANCE TO THIRST AND HUNGER

Dromedaries can go without food and water for **eight days** at a temperature of **122º F (50º C)**.

If all the hump's water is used up, it hangs off to one side of the body.

12% The maximum percentage of body weight a person can lose without dying

40% The maximum percentage of body weight camels can lose without dying

Record Breath-Holders

S perm whales are unique animals whose species is remarkable for many reasons. On the one hand, they have the ability to dive to a maximum depth of 9,800 feet (3,000 m) and remain underwater without oxygen for up to two hours. They are able to do this by means of a complex physiological mechanism that, for example, can decrease their heart rate, store and use air in the muscles, and prioritize the delivery of oxygen to certain vital organs such as the heart and lungs. They are the largest whales with teeth, which are found only on the lower mandible. ●

about 120 minutes

IS THE LENGTH OF TIME THEY CAN SPEND UNDERWATER WITHOUT BREATHING.

SPERM WHALE
Physeter catodon

Habitat	Deep waters
Status	Vulnerable
Sexual Maturity	18 years

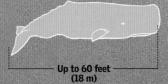

**Up to 60 feet
(18 m)**

Weight
20 to 90 tons

By Comparison
🐘🐘🐘🐘🐘🐘🐘🐘🐘🐘🐘
11 elephants of 8 tons apiece

1 SPIRACLE
The sperm whale breathes oxygen into its body through spiracles located on the top of its head.

2 REPRIORITIZING OXYGEN
Sperm whales can allocate oxygen to certain vital organs, such as the lungs and heart, directing it away from the digestive system.

MOUTH
Because of the placement of the nostrils, sperm whales can swim with their mouth open and capture prey. They feed on squid.

Spermaceti Organ

Sperm whales' ability to dive to great depths could be due in part to their spermaceti organ, located in their heads. It consists of a large mass of waxy oil that helps them both float and take deep dives. Its density changes with temperature and pressure change. It, like the melon of a dolphin, directs sound, focusing clicks, since its eyes are of little use when far from light.

Muscle

Spermaceti

Nostril

Mandibular Bone

Teeth
They have 18 to 20 conical teeth, weighing up to 2 pounds (1 kg) apiece, in each lower mandible.

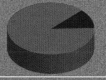

COMPOSITION
90% Spermaceti Oil
It is made up of esters and triglycerides.

Adaptation in Respiration

When they dive to great depths, sperm whales activate an entire physiological mechanism that makes maximum use of their oxygen reserves. This produces what is called a thoracic and pulmonary collapse, causing air to pass from the lungs to the trachea, reducing the absorption of the toxin nitrogen. They also rapidly transmit nitrogen from the blood to the lungs at the end of the dive, thus reducing the circulation of blood to the muscles. Sperm whales' muscles contain a large amount of myoglobin, a protein that stores oxygen, allowing the whales to stay underwater much longer.

ON THE SURFACE
Blowhole remains open, allowing the whales to breathe as much oxygen as they can before diving.

WHEN THEY DIVE
powerful muscles tightly close the opening of the blowhole, keeping water from entering.

BLOWHOLE
Upon submerging, it fills with water, which cools the spermaceti oil and makes it denser.

HEART
The heart rate slows down during the dive, limiting oxygen consumption.

BLOOD
An ample blood flow, rich in hemoglobin, transports elevated levels of oxygen to the body and brain.

RETIA MIRABILIA
The retia is a network of blood vessels (mirabilia) that filter the blood entering the brain.

LUNGS
absorb oxygen very efficiently.

TAIL
is large and horizontal and is the whale's main means of propulsion.

3 BRADYCARDIA
During a dive, the heart rate drops (a condition known as bradycardia), which lowers oxygen consumption.

Dive

True diving champions, sperm whales can dive to depths of 9,800 feet (3,000 m), descending up to 10 feet (3 m) per second in search of squid. As a general rule, their dives last about 50 minutes, but they can remain underwater up to two hours. Before beginning a deep dive, they lift their caudal fin completely out of the water. They do not have a dorsal fin, but they do have a few triangular humps on the posterior part of their body.

0 FEET (0 M)
ON THE SURFACE
They inhale oxygen through the blowhole located at the top of the head.

+ 3,300 FEET (1,000 M)
90 MINUTES
They store 90 percent of their oxygen in their muscles, so they can be submerged for a long time.

0 FEET (0 M)
ON THE SURFACE
They exhale all the air from their lungs; this is called spouting, or blowing.

Making Use of Oxygen

Sperm whales can dive deeper and stay submerged longer than any other mammal, because they have various ways of saving oxygen: an ability to store it in their muscles, a metabolism that can function anaerobically, and the inducement of bradycardia during a dive.

15%
AMOUNT OF AIR REPLACED IN ONE BREATH

85%
AMOUNT OF AIR REPLACED IN ONE BREATH

Aerial Acrobatics

C ats have a surprising ability to land upright. The secret lies in their skeleton, which is more flexible and has more bones than that of any other mammal. Cats' reflexes allow them to twist using the physical principle of the conservation of angular momentum. The principle, first formulated by Isaac Newton, states that all bodies in circular movement tend to a constant amount of energy. Thus, the more the animal extends its legs to its axis of rotation, the slower it rotates, redistributing the total energy of the system. If the animal tucks in its legs, it rotates more rapidly. ●

Name	Domestic cat
Family	Felidae
Species	*Felis catus*
Adult Weight	4 to 15 pounds (2-7 kg)
Longevity	15 years
Dimensions	

10 inches (25 cm)
12 inches (30 cm)
4 inches (10 cm)

FORCE OF GRAVITY

AXIS

1 STARTS UPSIDE DOWN
The cat begins to fall upside down and will turn 180º upon its axis (in two stages), landing upright.

2 FIRST TWIST
In this maneuver, the cat rotates the front half of its body 180º on its body's axis. The other half rotates only slightly as a result.

Strong Rotation

Slight Rotation

AXIS

Back Half

Front Half

3 WITH INDEPENDENCE
Like a skater who extends or folds the arms to control the speed of rotation, the cat moves its hind legs—but independently of each other.

The "Accelerator"
The cat folds its front legs in to its axis to increase the speed of rotation of this part. It rotates 180º.

The "Brake"
It extends its hind legs perpendicular to the axis and reduces the speed of rotation of this part.

It extends its front legs at right angles to the axis.

It draws its hind legs in to the axis of the body.

LIKE A SKATER

Radius

Axis

To reduce rotation
opens arms to increase the radius of rotation.

To increase rotation
closes arms to reduce the radius of the rotation.

Time of the Fall

A fall from a short distance usually causes more harm than one from a considerable height, because the cat adopts a defensive posture only when it senses acceleration in the fall. Upon reaching terminal velocity, it can accelerate no faster, and the cat relaxes, stretches out, and offers resistance to the fall.

○ Terminal velocity

Relaxation

Defensive posture

First twist

HEIGHT

HARM

Front Half
The extended legs reduce the speed of rotation of this part. It rotates 180°.

Back Half
Now the folded legs increase the speed of rotation of this part.

4 SECOND TWIST

The cat lowers its hind legs and completes a full rotation on its axis. It again carries out two more rotations, one tighter than the other:

Strong Rotation

AXIS

Slight Rotation

Front Half

Back Half

5 FOUR FEET PLACED UNDER THE BODY

With four feet positioned under the body, the cat bends its spine like a parachute and then merely corrects its posture for landing.

The tail stabilizes the weight of the body during the descent.

It extends the hind legs to the height of the front legs.

11% ELONGATION CAPACITY

Extreme Flexibility
Cats do not have a clavicle, and the articulations of their vertebrae are more flexible than those of most mammals. They can travel five times the length of their body in one leap.

1/8 of a second

TIME IT TAKES TO ROTATE AND LAND ON ITS FEET 1/2 SECOND LATER

6 LANDING

Its front legs make the first contact with the ground. Then it lands on its hind legs, and, finally, it relaxes its tail.

At the moment of landing, the cat slightly flexes its feet to cushion the blow.

Equilibrium

The inner ear in the temporal bone is divided into the cochlea, the vestibule, and three semicircular canals. Inside there is a system of cilia (sense receptors) and a viscous substance (endolymph) that generates the sense of balance when the two come in contact with each other.

Cross section of a semicircular canal

Bulla
It holds the cilia, which are equilibrium receptors.

During a rotation, endolymph moves the cilia in the direction opposite the body's motion.

QUICK AND PRECISE SHAKE
During the rotation, endolymph can splash into the semicircular canals. To return the liquid to its place, the cat gives a quick shake of its head.

INNER EAR

Cochlea

Nocturnal Flight

ats are the only mammals that can fly. Scientists call them Chiroptera, a term derived from Greek words meaning "winged hands." Their forelimbs have been transformed into hands with very long fingers joined together by a membrane (called the patagium) that forms the surface of the wing. These mammals' senses are so sensitive that they can move and hunt quickly and accurately in the dark. ●

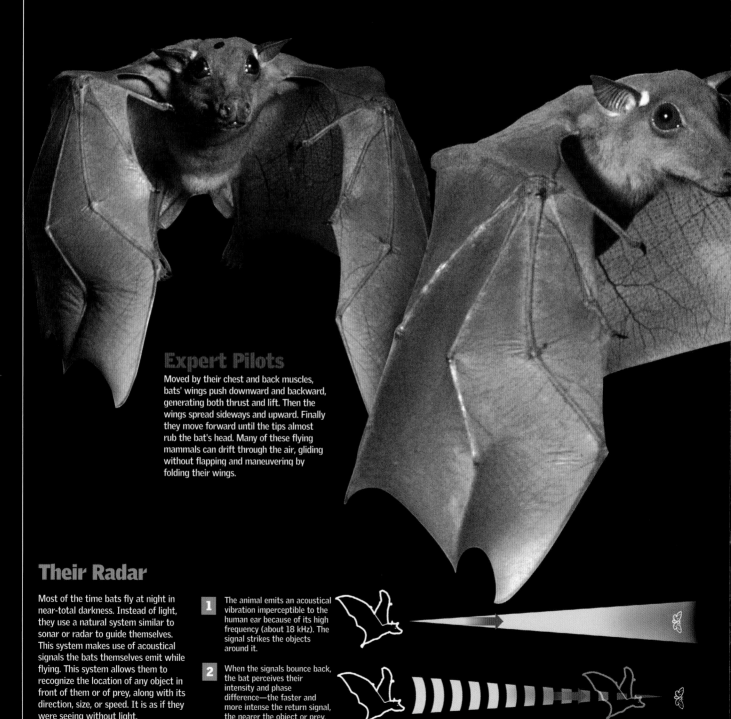

Expert Pilots

Moved by their chest and back muscles, bats' wings push downward and backward, generating both thrust and lift. Then the wings spread sideways and upward. Finally they move forward until the tips almost rub the bat's head. Many of these flying mammals can drift through the air, gliding without flapping and maneuvering by folding their wings.

Their Radar

Most of the time bats fly at night in near-total darkness. Instead of light, they use a natural system similar to sonar or radar to guide themselves. This system makes use of acoustical signals the bats themselves emit while flying. This system allows them to recognize the location of any object in front of them or of prey, along with its direction, size, or speed. It is as if they were seeing without light.

1 The animal emits an acoustical vibration imperceptible to the human ear because of its high frequency (about 18 kHz). The signal strikes the objects around it.

2 When the signals bounce back, the bat perceives their intensity and phase difference—the faster and more intense the return signal, the nearer the object or prey.

60 miles per hour (97 km)

THE SPEED SOME BATS MAY REACH DURING FLIGHT

Hibernation

These bats spend the winter in a lethargic state hanging by their feet, faces down, in caves and other dark places. Bats are warm-blooded animals while they are active and become similar to cold-blooded creatures when they are asleep. They enter into a state of hibernation more rapidly and easily than any other mammal, and they can survive in cold temperatures for many months—even inside refrigerators—without needing to feed.

FRUIT BAT (FRANQUET'S EPAULETTED BAT)
Epomops franqueti

Habitat	Forests of Ghana and Congo
Family	Pteropodae
Length of wingspan	14 inches (36 cm)

HUMERUS

RADIUS

THUMB

SECOND FINGER

FOURTH FINGER

THIRD FINGER

PATAGIUM

1
2
3
4
5

HAND OR WING
The first finger, or thumb, has no membrane and is used as a claw. Powerful muscles move the entire wing.

UROPATAGIUM

ELASTIC FIBERS
The texture of the wing is soft and flexible. It is lined with blood vessels.

Flexible Wings

The patagium is formed by the membranes between the digits. In some species, the wings are also extended by an additional membrane (uropatagium), which joins the hind limbs to the tail. Their wings are not only used for flying (pushing the air as if they were oars in water) but also help to maintain a constant body temperature and to trap insects, upon which bats feed.

Playing Hide and Seek

ust like other species of the animal kingdom, some mammals that live in the wild rely on their bodies' colorations or appearances to disguise their presence. Some mammals imitate objects in their environment, and others take on the appearances of other animals. Zebras' stripes, for example, give these animals a very showy appearance—but when moving in their natural environment, zebras are camouflaged. Some differentiate between mimicry and crypsis, which is the natural ability to go unnoticed without requiring any associated behavior. In other cases, however, the forms and colors of camouflage would be useless if they were not accompanied by some kind of imitative behavior. An animal cannot improve its camouflage, but it can improve its mimicry.

Evolutionary Adaptations

Mimicry is defined as the ability of some living beings to imitate the appearance of another living being or an inanimate object in the environment. Protective mimicry is the camouflage used by animals incapable of defending themselves in any other way. Aggressive mimicry, on the other hand, allows organisms to surprise and attack their prey. This occurs, for example, with wild felines (mountain lions, ocelots, lynxes), which take advantage of their skin colors and the patterns of their fur to go unnoticed in their ecosystems. Zebras travel in herds as a natural form of self-protection. The disruptive coloration of their coats makes it difficult for predators that rely on speed and sharp senses to distinguish one individual prey from another. Kicking and biting, zebras collectively defend themselves from attacks by feline predators. These felines also make use of camouflage strategies to make their attacks one on one. Many animals make use of elements from their surroundings or even of other living organisms to camouflage themselves. Sloths are another example; being the slowest of the mammals, they have no choice but to cover themselves in algae to avoid notice.

STRIPES
The coloration of their coat changes with the incidence and intensity of sunlight.

SPOTS
allow giraffes to conceal themselves among the high leaves they reach with their long neck.

PATTERNS
are irregular forms between stripes that allow tigers to lie in ambush for their prey among thickets.

Different Patterns

The pattern of a zebra's coat does not exactly copy the shapes and colors of objects in the wild environment surrounding it. Nevertheless, it does have patterns that allow it, with the help of certain behaviors and motions, to disguise its appearance in more than one setting of the zebra's natural habitat. In the case of Arctic animals, it is the uniform white color of the winter environment that determines the way in which species camouflage themselves.

In Motion

The patterns of tigers' coats are useful in concealing their contours, especially when they are moving among the shrubs and bushes of the plains where they hunt. Elk horns, however, can be concealed among the vegetation they resemble only so long as they keep still.

Disruptive Coloration

The body's contours are blurred when some spots of color are much darker or lighter than the rest of the coat.

Part of the Hideaway

Chipmunks (*Tamias* species) live in coniferous or deciduous forests, where they feed on nuts, insects, eggs, seeds, and other plant foods. The colors of their coats are essential, because—although they are very skillful at moving in the upper branches—their small size and short legs make them very vulnerable when they are on the ground.

PROTECTIVE SURROUNDINGS
Many have a coat that changes color depending on the surroundings.

FUR
Shades and differences of color in the coat are similar to those of tree trunks and dry leaves.

The Language of Water

he ways in which cetaceans communicate with others of their kind are among the most sophisticated in the animal kingdom. Dolphins, for example, click with their mandibles when in trouble and whistle repeatedly when afraid or excited. During courtship and mating, they touch and caress. They also communicate through visual signals—such as leaping—to show that food is close by. They have a wide variety of ways to transmit important information.

HAVING FUN
Play for dolphins, as with other mammals, fulfills an essential role in the formation of social strata.

Common Name	Bottlenose dolphin
Family	Delphinidae
Species	*Tursiops truncatus*
Adult Weight	330 to 1,400 pounds (150 to 650 kg)
Longevity	30 to 40 years

7 to 13 feet (2-4 m)

They reach
**22 mph
(35 km/h)**

MELON
is an organ filled with low-density lipids that concentrate and direct the pulses emitted, sending waves forward. The shape of the melon can be varied to better focus the sounds.

SPIRACLE **LIP**

NASAL AIR SAC

DORSAL FIN
allows dolphins to maintain their equilibrium in the water.

INHALATION
The spiracle opens so oxygen can enter.

Spiracle

Air to the lungs

HOW THE SOUND IS PRODUCED

LARYNX

2 The nasal air sacs begin to inflate.

They can go 12 minutes without taking in oxygen.

CAUDAL FIN
has a horizontal axis (unlike that of fish), which serves to propel dolphins forward.

4 The nasal air sacs deflate

Melon

Air in the lungs

1 Emission
Sounds are generated by air passing through the respiratory chambers. But it is in the melon that resonance is generated and amplified. Greater frequencies and intensities are achieved in this way.

3 EXHALATION
Air resonates in the nasal sacs and is emitted under pressure through the spiracle.

Brain

PECTORAL FIN

MANDIBLE
The lower mandible plays a very important role in the transmission of sounds to the inner ear.

③ Reception and Interpretation

The middle ear sends the message to the brain. Dolphins hear frequencies from 100 Hz up to 150 kHz (the human ear can hear only up to 15 kHz). Low-frequency signals (whistles, snores, grunts, clinking) are key in the social life of dolphins, cetaceans that cannot live alone.

3 pounds
(1.4 kg)
HUMAN BRAIN

4 pounds
(1.7 kg)
DOLPHIN BRAIN

MORE NEURONS
A dolphin's brain, which processes the signals, has at least double the convolutions of those of humans, as well as nearly 50 percent more neurons.

MIDDLE EAR

② Message

Low-frequency signals are used for communication with other dolphins, and high-frequency signals are used as sonar.

1 mile per second
(1.5 km/s)

SOUND WAVES TRAVEL 4.5 TIMES FASTER IN WATER THAN IN AIR.

Echolocation

A The dolphin emits a series of **clicking** sounds from the nasal cavity.

B The melon concentrates the clicks and projects them forward.

C These waves bounce off objects they encounter in their way.

E The intensity, pitch, and return time of the echo indicate the size, position, and direction of the obstacle.

D Part of the signal bounces back and returns to the dolphin in the form of an echo.

SIGNAL WITH ECHO

Click | Echo | Click | Echo

0 s | 6 s | 12 s | 18 s

Lively Tunnels

Rabbits are gregarious animals that live in colonies in a series of burrows called warrens. The burrows are dug underground and are inhabited by females of high social rank. Rabbits are principally nocturnal and spend most of the day hidden in the burrow, leaving to eat when night falls. ●

PREFERRED PLACES
The area around the burrow needs two things before the rabbits will feel comfortable—grass and cover. Generally rabbits build warrens in meadows near thickets or rocks.

HIND FOOT

Danger Print — Normal Footprint

200 feet
(60 m)
IS THE FARTHEST A RABBIT WILL WILLINGLY GO FROM ITS BURROW.

RABBIT FOOTPRINTS
Their footprints are unmistakable, the result of their peculiar way of walking and jumping.

ENTRANCE TO THE WARREN
6 inches (15 cm)

In the presence of strangers or in other cases of danger, rabbits thump the ground with the back part of their hind feet, warning the others not to leave the burrow.

When they thump, rabbits produce a sound that all the rabbits in the colony hear. If a rabbit is trapped, it will emit a sharp squeal that can be heard throughout the area.

Warren
This is the main part of the burrow, where the adult rabbits live. It is made up of a complex network of interconnected corridors and chambers.

MOUNDS

FOOD DEPOSIT

NEST

PROTECTED INTERIOR
Interior tunnels are lined with vegetation and rabbit fur to keep them from deteriorating and to protect them from moisture.

Rabbits that receive the warning will remain in place, motionless.

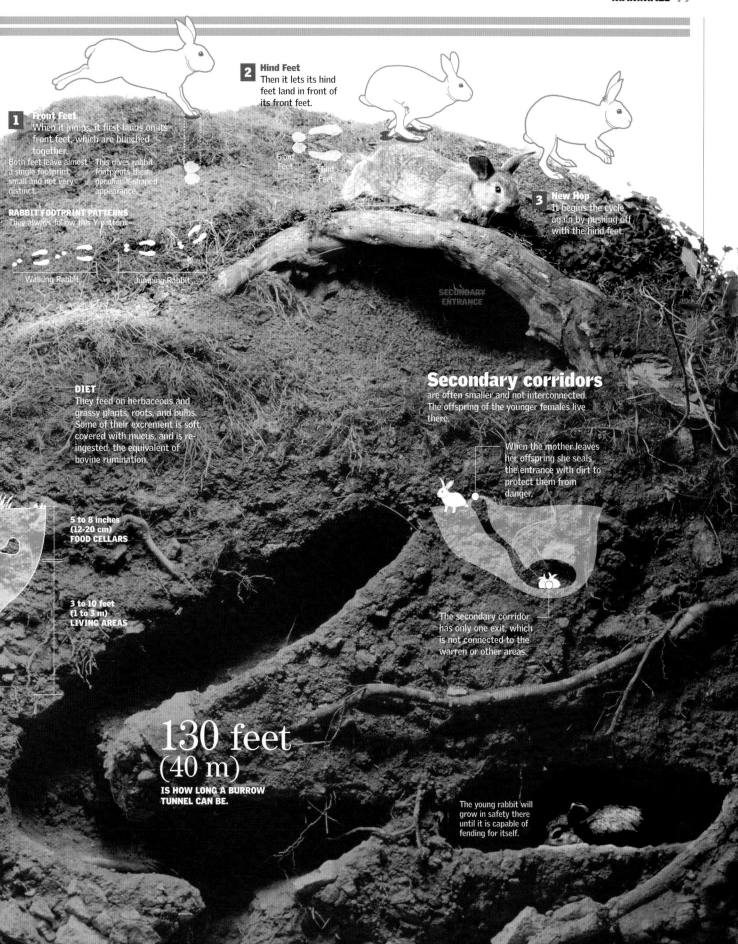

1 **Front Feet**
When it jumps, it first lands on its front feet, which are bunched together.

Both feet leave almost a single footprint, small and not very distinct.

This gives rabbit footprints their peculiar Y-shaped appearance.

2 **Hind Feet**
Then it lets its hind feet land in front of its front feet.

Front Feet

Hind Feet

3 **New Hop**
It begins the cycle again by pushing off with the hind feet.

RABBIT FOOTPRINT PATTERNS
They always follow this Y pattern.

Walking Rabbit

Jumping Rabbit

DIET
They feed on herbaceous and grassy plants, roots, and bulbs. Some of their excrement is soft, covered with mucus, and is re-ingested, the equivalent of bovine rumination.

SECONDARY ENTRANCE

Secondary corridors
are often smaller and not interconnected. The offspring of the younger females live there.

When the mother leaves her offspring she seals the entrance with dirt to protect them from danger.

5 to 8 inches
(12-20 cm)
FOOD CELLARS

3 to 10 feet
(1 to 3 m)
LIVING AREAS

The secondary corridor has only one exit, which is not connected to the warren or other areas.

130 feet
(40 m)
IS HOW LONG A BURROW TUNNEL CAN BE.

The young rabbit will grow in safety there until it is capable of fending for itself.

Relationship with People

The history of cats goes back 12 million years to the time when felines began to populate the Earth. However, their domestication began 4,000 years ago. The Egyptians decided to incorporate them into their home life, thus keeping rats away. Then the Phoenicians took them to Italy and the rest of Europe. One of the subjects

LIKABLE AND PLAYFUL
Cats are excellent companion animals and are known for their great independence and cleanliness.

discussed in this chapter has to do with the things that threaten the existence of many animal species, including the loss of natural habitats, poaching, pollution, and illegal pet trafficking. Within the next 30 years, almost one fourth of the Earth's mammals could disappear. ●

Myths and Legends

Human history has always been intimately linked with the various mammals—after all, people are mammals, too! Numerous myths and legends have arisen from this relationship, such as that of the wolf goddess Luperca, who saved Romulus and Remus from death—or the story of the birth of the Minotaur, in which a queen was caused to fall hopelessly in love with a bull and give birth to a monster with a bull's head and man's body. The origin of each myth springs from a particular tradition and means something different in each culture.

PEGASUS

Winged horse, son of Medusa, who flew to Olympus and was received by Zeus. Thereafter, he transported thunderbolts for the king of the gods, who placed his figure in the night sky.

TROJAN HORSE

Unable to capture the city of Troy during a siege that lasted 10 years, the Greeks built a hollow wooden horse, concealed warriors inside it, and left it on the beach. The Trojans, thinking it a gift from Poseidon, brought it into the city. At night, the warriors left their hiding place and opened the city's gates to the remainder of the Greek army, burning and seizing the city.

West

In Western culture, the Greeks and Romans have been the great producers of myths and legends relating animals to humans. Human bodies with the heads of bulls or the limbs of horses are some of many examples.

CERBERUS

This was the monstrous, three-headed hound of Hades, or hellhound, which guarded the kingdom of the dead, preventing the dead from leaving and the living from entering.

MINOTAUR
In Greek mythology, this was a creature born with the body of a man and the head of a bull that ate human flesh. It was born on the island of Crete of a forced sexual relationship between Pasiphae, wife of King Minos, and a white bull that Poseidon gave the king to use as a sacrifice.

East
In Eastern culture, animals, especially mammals, have played a leading role in myths and legends. Sometimes one animal has various meanings in various cultures. To Egyptians, cats represent harmony and happiness, but the Buddhist world disapproves of cats because they, along with snakes, were the only ones who did not cry at Buddha's death.

UNICORN
This stone seal depicting a unicorn is found in the National Museum of Pakistan in Karachi and dates from the year 2300 BC.

LION
The Manjusri Buddha, seated on the mythical lion who is the guardian of Buddhist doctrine

Myths
THEIR ORIGIN STEMS FROM THE OBSERVATION OF NATURE.

ROMULUS AND REMUS
These two brothers were abandoned on the shores of the Tiber, but they were found by a female wolf, Luperca, who suckled and raised them. Later, as adults, they returned to the place where they had been abandoned and there founded Rome.

CAT
Bastet, the Egyptian goddess who watched over the home. She symbolizes the joy of living and was represented as a woman with a cat's head, because her sacred animal was the cat.

Each in Its Place

ature takes care of maintaining its equilibrium, providing each animal its own role within the food chain. When one of the roles is removed, equilibrium in the region is lost. In Australia, dingoes were a big problem for sheep farmers, who built a great fence to protect their flocks. This barrier left the wild dogs without prey and other species able to move about more freely in search of food. Dingoes are classified as pests both for farm animals as well as for rabies control.

The Introduction of the Dingo

It is thought that dingoes were domesticated animals of the Australian Aborigines who lived in the region. These mammals originated in Asia and were brought to Australia by humans. They are medium-sized wild dogs with thick tails and are notable for having a very distinctive howl instead of a bark. When European pioneers arrived in Australia, dingoes were accepted, but this rapidly changed when sheep became an important part of the economy. Dingoes were soon trapped, hunted, and poisoned.

CHAIN
Because of the building of the barrier, herbivorous animals have more space to graze, safe from the presence of dingoes.

DINGO
The leading predators of sheep, dingoes were isolated from the area.

SHEEP
Their population increased with the absence of the dingo.

KANGAROO
They found greater freedom to move about in search of food.

PASTURELANDS
became scarce, making it difficult for herbivores such as kangaroos and sheep to find food.

DINGO
Canis dingo

The Great Fence

 was designed to keep dingoes out of the southeastern part of Australia, protecting flocks of sheep. It ran for thousands of miles and was largely successful in its objective. The number of dingoes in the area declined, and, although the loss of sheep to predators was reduced, this decline led to an ecological imbalance by increasing the competition for pastureland among rabbits and kangaroos.

3,300 miles
(5,320 km)
THE LENGTH OF THE GREAT FENCE.

— ORIGINAL COURSE

CURRENT COURSE ● AREA FREE OF DINGOES

AUSTRALIA

SYDNEY

MELBOURNE

Its shape changes according to its upkeep. The Australian government subsidizes the undertaking, but sheep farmers are the ones who maintain it.

Wool Industry

Australia is second in the world in wool production. It has 110 million sheep within its borders, constituting 10 percent of world wool production. In 1989, when part of the famous fence collapsed, about 20,000 sheep were lost to dingoes.

Raising Hogs

Hog farming is one of the oldest forms of livestock production. In fact, the biggest hog producers, the Chinese, began raising hogs more than 7,000 years ago. But raising hogs has become more and more complex. Today, to produce large litters and high-quality pork as quickly as possible, pigs are crossbred. ●

Pork Production

The use of genetics in a pig nursery is complex and important because breeds of pigs are very specific. Here are the most notable differences among various breeds.

MEAT BREEDS have high weight gain, a good build, and a high food-conversion efficiency.

Hampshire

Duroc

Pietrain

MATERNAL BREEDS They are very prolific, have good maternal skills, and produce a large number of piglets.

Landrace

Yorkshire

CROSS TO OBTAIN A HOG FOR CONSUMPTION

100% Meat breed ♂
100% Maternal breed ♀

50% Meat breed 50% Maternal breed ♂
100% Maternal breed ♀

100% Meat breed ♂
75% Maternal breed 25% Meat breed ♀

FAT
62.5% Meat breed
37.5% Maternal breed

① Mountings

Older sows coming from the breeding room and young replacement gilts enter pens where they will be naturally or artificially impregnated.

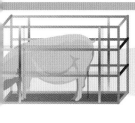

210 to 220 pounds
(95-100 kg)

IS THE WEIGHT OF A PIG
WHEN IT IS READY TO BE
SLAUGHTERED.

② Gestation

Once impregnated, they are taken to the gestation room, where they will remain for 114 days, or until two or three days before giving birth. To prevent problems when they give birth, they receive a restricted diet so they do not get fat.

③ Maternity

They give birth to litters of 10 to 12 animals and can produce over 3 gallons (12 l) of milk daily. Feeding is unrestricted so that the sow is not left weakened after weaning.

④ Raising

The recently weaned piglets enter nursery crates kept at an ambient temperature averaging 77º F (25° C). They are given an initial ration and remain here from day 21 to day 45.

⑤ Fattening

This period lasts approximately 90 days. When the pigs are 150 days old, they weigh about 210 pounds (95 kg).

⑥ Slaughter

Once they weigh between 210 and 220 pounds (95-100 kg), the pigs are transferred to the slaughterhouse. There they are given an electric shock that renders them unconscious before they are killed. They are scalded in hot water to detach their hair, are bled, and are then eviscerated, and the carcass is prepared for final butchering.

The Cuts

The animal can be sold as a dressed carcass or in pieces and taken to supermarkets. Its meat will be used to make sausages or left as entire cuts.

BACON   LOIN AND CHOP   TAIL

FOOT

SHOULDER   RIBS   HAM
BLADE

FEED
It is common to use growth hormones to increase food conversion efficiency and the lean-meat content in the dressed carcass.

Milk Production

Until the 18th century, milk was a little-consumed product because it could be kept for only a few hours without spoiling. It was not easy to offer a supply of fresh milk to meet urban needs. Only in the 20th century, after the discovery of pasteurization, allowing milk to be preserved, did milk become a universally popular drink produced industrially. ●

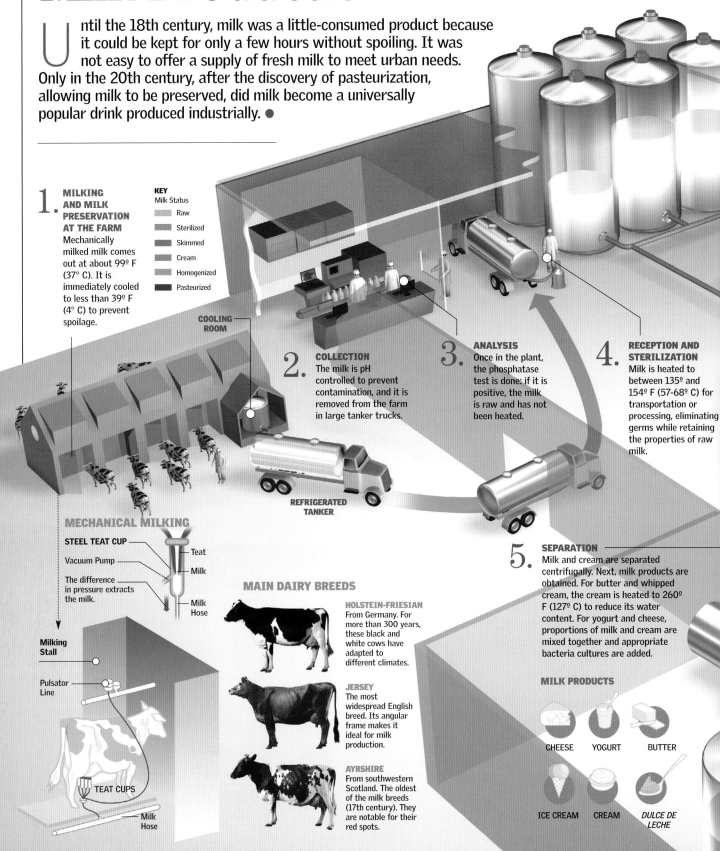

1. MILKING AND MILK PRESERVATION AT THE FARM
Mechanically milked milk comes out at about 99º F (37° C). It is immediately cooled to less than 39º F (4° C) to prevent spoilage.

KEY
Milk Status
- Raw
- Sterilized
- Skimmed
- Cream
- Homogenized
- Pasteurized

COOLING ROOM

2. COLLECTION
The milk is pH controlled to prevent contamination, and it is removed from the farm in large tanker trucks.

3. ANALYSIS
Once in the plant, the phosphatase test is done: if it is positive, the milk is raw and has not been heated.

4. RECEPTION AND STERILIZATION
Milk is heated to between 135º and 154º F (57-68º C) for transportation or processing, eliminating germs while retaining the properties of raw milk.

REFRIGERATED TANKER

MECHANICAL MILKING

STEEL TEAT CUP — Teat
Vacuum Pump — Milk
The difference in pressure extracts the milk. — Milk Hose

Milking Stall
Pulsator Line
TEAT CUPS
Milk Hose

MAIN DAIRY BREEDS

HOLSTEIN-FRIESIAN
From Germany. For more than 300 years, these black and white cows have adapted to different climates.

JERSEY
The most widespread English breed. Its angular frame makes it ideal for milk production.

AYRSHIRE
From southwestern Scotland. The oldest of the milk breeds (17th century). They are notable for their red spots.

5. SEPARATION
Milk and cream are separated centrifugally. Next, milk products are obtained. For butter and whipped cream, the cream is heated to 260º F (127° C) to reduce its water content. For yogurt and cheese, proportions of milk and cream are mixed together and appropriate bacteria cultures are added.

MILK PRODUCTS

CHEESE   YOGURT   BUTTER

ICE CREAM   CREAM   *DULCE DE LECHE*

6. **HOMOGENIZATION** ensures that the product is uniform in consistency. It consists of the dispersion of the milk's fat globules by means of friction created under very high pressure.

High-pressure streams of milk collide with a piston, reducing the size of the fat particles.

Milk Pipeline
Piston
Smaller Particles

HOMOGENIZER

WATER HEATER

7. **PASTEURIZATION** ensures that potentially harmful microorganisms are eliminated from the milk but does not change the milk's properties. It begins with rapid heating from a source of indirect heat, followed by circulation through a cold pipe for quick cooling.

HEATING   COOLING

Milk Entrance

Hot Water 162º F   Cold Water 39º F
(72° C)   (4° C)

Louis Pasteur
1822-95
French chemist. Among other things, he discovered that the decomposition of food is caused by bacteria, and he invented the first ways to keep substances from spoiling.

8. **BOTTLING** Peroxide solutions are used to sterilize the containers, and reagent strips are used to ensure that no peroxide residue remains.

CONTROL ROOM
The various steps of the processes carried out in modern plants are automated and controlled by computers from a central office.

HEAT EXCHANGE

Skim Milk Tank

Pasteurized, Homogenized Milk Tank

SEPARATOR

PACKER

SEALING MACHINE
is maintained in aseptic conditions. Processing and expiration dates are stamped on the container.

Internal layers of the separator where cream particles are decanted as grainy sediment

Cream Tanks

ANNUAL PRODUCTION OF FRESH MILK

140 billion gallons

FILLING MACHINE
Except in the case of long-life milk, the machine fills containers that will allow the milk to be preserved for two weeks under adequately cold conditions.

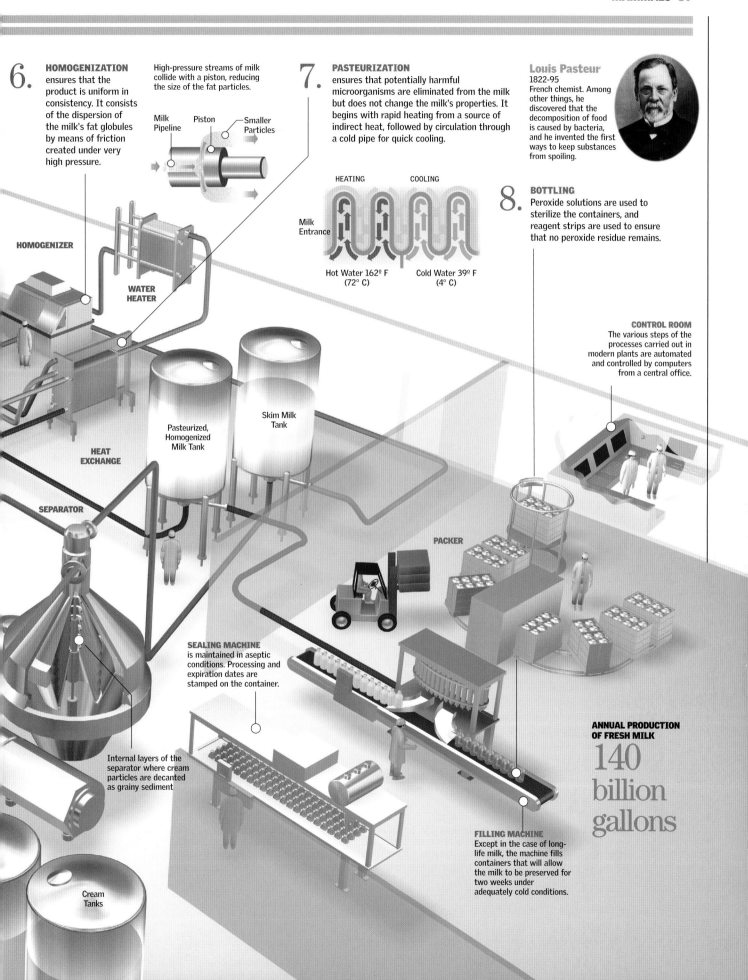

The Human Threat

O ver the next 30 years, almost a quarter of the mammals could disappear from the face of the Earth, according to the United Nations. The eminent collapse reflects an unequivocally human stamp: hunting, deforestation, pollution, urbanization, and massive tourism. Experts calculate that more than 1,000 mammals are endangered or vulnerable, and 20 areas of the planet have been identified where probabilities of extinction may exist in the near future. ●

Affected Regions

There are 781 threatened species in the region of sub-Saharan Africa, and in South Asia there are 726. South America contains another 346 endangered species, and Central and North America have 63 endangered mammals.

MAMMALS OF THE WORLD

More than one out of every five species of mammals is endangered: 20 to 25 percent of existing mammalian species.

1,097 Threatened species

4,319 Species that are not threatened or for which there is no information

162 Critical

583 Vulnerable

348 Endangered

ENDANGERED BY COUNTRY

Indonesia has the most endangered species, followed by the "country of tigers," India. In Latin America, Brazil is first and Mexico second.

Country	Value
Indonesia	135
India	80
Brazil	75
China	72
Cameroon	39
Tanzania	38
Russian Federation	35
Thailand	32
U.S.	29

5,416
IS THE NUMBER OF EXISTING MAMMAL SPECIES.

NORTH AMERICA

CENTRAL AMERICA

Atlantic Ocean

Pacific Ocean

SOUTH AMERICA

EUROPE

AFRICA

Sea Otter
Enhydra lutris

Once a continuous line of sea otter colonies stretched from the Kuril Islands of Japan to California. Today only a few colonies remain in Alaska and in the lower United States.

Dama Gazelle

The degradation of their habitat, as well as unregulated hunting, threaten their existence. In the Sahara, their population fell by 80 percent in only 10 years.

Southern Right Whale
Eubalaena australis

inhabits a broad band extending from 20º S to 60º S. They are sought for their high quantities of body oils, and they are relatively easy to capture. It is estimated that only 3,000 exist today.

Chinchilla
Chinchilla brevicaudata
They live in the Andes Mountains of Chile and Peru. Indiscriminate hunting has decreased the species, and it is endangered.

Cetaceans

Gray whales, which inhabit the waters of the northern Pacific and the Arctic, are protected. In 1970, sperm whales were declared endangered, and today hunting them is prohibited. The Indian Ocean has been declared a whale sanctuary in an effort to curb hunting, but 7 out of 13 great whales remain in danger of extinction, as do a similar number of dolphin species.

DEGREE OF THREAT

Extinct	Has not been seen for 30 years
In the Wild	Survives in captivity
Critically Endangered	500 individuals
Endangered	1,000 to 2,000 individuals
Vulnerable	Up to 5,000 individuals

KEY

- MAMMALS AT CRITICAL RISK
- ○ UP TO 10 SPECIES ALREADY EXTINCT
- MORE THAN 10 SPECIES ALREADY EXTINCT

Families of Primates

Twenty-five percent of the 625 species and subspecies of primates are in danger of extinction. The principal causes are deforestation, indiscriminate commercial hunting, and illegal trafficking of animals. In the countries of Gabon and Congo, where the majority of chimpanzees and gorillas live, the population decreased by more than half between 1983 and 2000.

FAMILY HYLOBATIDAE

Gibbon   Siamang

FAMILY PONGIDAE

Gorilla   Chimpanzee

Titi   Orangutan

ASIA

IUCN
The World Conservation Union

The World Conservation Union was created in 1948, bringing together 81 nations and nearly 10,000 specialists.

Pacific Ocean

Hippopotamus

These are among the most vulnerable animals. From 1994 until today, their population in Zambia and the Democratic Republic of Congo has fallen by 95 percent.

Indian Ocean

Orangutans

Pongo pygmaeuspygmaeus (Borneo)
Pongo pygmaeus abelii (Sumatra)

Found in the tropical forests of the islands of Borneo and Sumatra. Indiscriminate logging, mining, and forest fires isolate them from nature, as does the illegal capture of their young, which are then sold as pets.

Hainan Black-crested Gibbon
Nomascus nasutus sp. *hainanus*
These primates are among the five species in most danger of extinction. Only 30 black-crested gibbons are known to exist.

OCEANIA

Dolphin

Harbor Porpoise

Sperm Whale

Blue Whale

Gray Whale

Fin Whale

Giant Panda
Ailuropoda melanoleuca

One thousand bears survive in reserves created in China. The disappearance of their habitat—caused by the felling of bamboo, their natural food—as well as the extreme difficulty they have reproducing in captivity (because of their timidity) are the principal reasons for the decrease in this species.

Glossary

Abomasum

Last of the four chambers into which ruminants' stomachs are divided. It secretes strong acids and many digestive enzymes.

Agouti

Rodent mammal of South America measuring approximately 20 inches (50 cm) and having large feet, a short tail, and small ears.

Albumin

Protein found in abundance in blood plasma. It is the principal protein in the blood and is synthesized in the liver. It is also found in egg whites and in milk.

Alveolar Gland

Functional production unit in which a single layer of milk-secreting cells is spherically grouped, having a central depression called a lumen.

Biome

Land or water ecosystem with a certain type of predominant vegetation and fauna.

Biped

Adjective applied to species of mammals that walk on two feet.

Bradychardia

Lowering of cardiac frequency to below 60 beats per minute in humans.

Bunny

This is a young or growing rabbit.

Carnassial

A typical sharp premolar present in carnivorous animals that helps them cut and tear the flesh of their prey more efficiently.

Carpus

Bone structure of the wrist, located between the bones of the forearm and the metacarpus. It is made up of two rows of bones.

Chiridium

A muscular limb in tetrapods. It is a long bone whose anterior end articulates with the scapular belt. The posterior end articulates with two bones that connect to the joints of the digits.

Cloaca

The open chamber into which the ducts of the urinary and reproductive systems empty.

Cochlea

A structure shaped like a coiled spiral tube, located in the inner ear of mammals.

Concha

The arched, osseous plate found in each of the nostrils.

Cones

The photoreceptor cells in the retina of vertebrates. They are essential for distinguishing colors.

Convolution

Each of the slight elevations or folds that mark the surface of the cerebral cortex.

Cortex

The outer tissue of some organs, such as the brain and kidney.

Counter Shading

The characteristic of protective coloration in the hair or fur of certain mammals that are dorsally dark and ventrally lighter.

Cynodonts

Animals that, beginning in the Triassic Period, start to exhibit characteristics essential to the lives of warm-blooded animals, making them relatives of true mammals. They include the Mammaliaformes.

Dendrite

The branched elongation of a nerve cell by means of which it receives external stimuli.

Dermis

The inner layer of the skin, located under the epidermis.

Dichromatic

Refers to mammals, such as mice and dogs, that have two types of cones in their retinas and can only distinguish certain colors.

Digitigrade

Refers to animals that use only their digits to walk. One example is dogs.

Dimorphism

Two anatomical forms in the same species. Sexual dimorphism is common between males and females of the same species.

Domestication

The process by which an animal population adapts to human beings and captivity through a series of genetic changes that occur over time, as well as by means of adaptation processes brought about and repeated over generations.

Echolocation

The ability to orient and maneuver by emitting sounds and interpreting their echoes.

Ecosystem

A dynamic system formed by a group of interrelated living beings and their environment.

Embryo

A living being in the first stages of its development, from fertilization until it acquires the characteristic appearance of its species.

Endemism

The characteristic of a specific area where animal or plant species are natively and exclusively found.

Endothermy

The ability to regulate metabolism to maintain a constant body temperature independent of the ambient temperature.

Epidermis

The outer layer of the skin formed by epithelial tissue covering the bodies of animals.

Erythrocyte

A spherical blood cell containing hemoglobin, which gives blood its characteristic red color and transports oxygen throughout the body. It is also known as a red blood cell.

Estrus

The period of heat, or greatest sexual receptivity, of the female.

Ethology

The science that studies animal behavior.

Eumelanin

One of the types of melanin, a darkish brown color pigment.

Eutheria

One of the infraclasses into which the Theria subclass is divided, applied to animals that complete their development in the placenta.

Fetlock Joint

In quadrupeds, the limb joint between the cannon bone and the pastern.

Follicle

A small organ in the form of a sac located in the skin or mucous membranes.

Gestation

The state of an embryo inside a woman or female mammal from conception until birth.

Glomerulus

A ball-shaped structure such as the renal glomeruli, which are formed by a tiny ball of capillaries and which filter the blood.

Habitat

The set of geophysical conditions in which an individual species or a community of animals or plants lives.

Hibernation

The physiological state that occurs in certain mammals as an adaptation to extreme winter conditions, exhibited as a drop in body temperature and a general decrease in metabolic function.

Hock

The joint located between the metatarsal and tarsal bones of the hind limbs of a quadruped.

Homeostasis

The set of self-regulating phenomena that keeps the composition and properties of an organism's internal environment constant.

Homeothermy

Thermoregulation characteristic of animals that maintain a constant internal temperature, regardless of external conditions. Body temperature is usually higher than that of the immediate environment.

Hoof

Horny, or cornified, covering that completely envelops the distal extremity of horses' feet.

Iris

The membranous disk of the eye between the cornea and the lens that can take on different coloration. In its center is the pupil, which is dilated and contracted by the muscle fibers of the iris.

Keratin

A protein rich in sulfur, it constitutes the chief element of the outermost layers of mammals' epidermises, including hair, horns, nails, and hooves. It is the source of their strength and hardness.

Lactation

The period in mammals' lives when they feed solely on maternal milk.

Litter

All the offspring of a mammal born at one time.

Mammaliaformes

See Cynodonts.

Mammalogy

The science of studying mammals.

Mammary Gland

One of a pair of external secretion organs characteristic of mammals. It provides milk to the young during lactation.

Marsupial

Mammals whose females give birth to unviable infants, which are then incubated in the ventral pouch, where the mammary glands are located. They belong to the Metatheria infraclass.

Marsupium

The pouch, characteristic of female marsupials, that functions as an incubation chamber. It is formed by a fold of the skin and is attached to the outer ventral wall. The mammary glands are found there, and the offspring complete the gestation period there.

Melanin

The black or blackish-brown pigment found in the protoplasm of certain cells. It gives coloration to the skin, hair, choroid membranes, and so on.

Metacarpus

The set of elongated bones that make up the skeleton of the anterior limbs of certain animals and of the human hand. They are articulated to the bones of the carpus, or wrist, and the phalanges.

Metatheria

The infraclass of the Theria subclass, it contains species that reproduce partially inside the mother and then continue their development inside the marsupium.

Molt

The process by which certain animals shed their skin or feathers; or, when plants shed their foliage.

Monotremata

The only order of the Prototheria subclass, it consists of egg-laying mammals with a marsupium in which they incubate their eggs. The mammary glands are tubular and similar to sweat glands. They are distributed in four families, half of which are now extinct.

Multituberculate

A group of mammals that lived predominantly during the Mesozoic Era and that became extinct during the early part of the Cenozoic Era.

Neuron

A differentiated cell of the nervous system capable of transmitting nerve impulses among other neurons. It is composed of a receptor site, dendrites, and a transmission (or release) site—the axon, or neurite.

Nostril

Each of the openings of the nasal cavities that lead to the outside of the body.

Omasum

A ruminant's third stomach chamber. It is a small organ with a high absorptive capacity. It permits the recycling of water and minerals such as sodium and phosphorus, which may return to the rumen through the saliva.

Oviduct

The duct through which the ova leave the ovary to be fertilized.

Oviparous

Refers to animals that lay eggs outside the mother's body, where they complete their development before hatching.

Papilla

Each of the small, conical elevations on skin or mucous membranes, especially those on the tongue, by means of which the sense of taste functions.

Pasteur, Louis

(1822-95) The French chemist who developed pasteurization and other scientific advances.

Pasteurization

The process that ensures the destruction of pathogenic bacteria and the reduction of benign flora in milk without significantly affecting its physicochemical properties.

Patagium

The very fine membrane that joins the fingers and anterior limbs with the body, feet, and tail of bats.

Pheomelanin

One of the types of melanin, a yellowish-red pigment.

Pheromone

A volatile chemical substance produced by the sexual glands and used to attract an individual for reproductive purposes.

Phylogeny

The origin and evolutionary development of species and, generally, genealogies of living beings.

Placenta

The spongy tissue that completely surrounds the embryo and whose function is to allow the exchange of substances through the blood. It also protects the fetus from infections and controls physiological processes during gestation and birth.

Placentalia

The name by which the species in the Eutheria infraclass orders are also known.

Plantigrade

Refers to mammals that use the entire foot in walking. Humans are plantigrade.

Polyandry

Refers to the relationship in which a female copulates with various males during one breeding period.

Polyestrous

Refers to an animal that has multiple annual breeding, or reproductive, periods.

Polygyny

The social system of certain animals, in which the male gathers a harem of females.

Prototheria

A subclass of the mammal class, it has a single order, Monotremata.

Quadruped

Refers to a four-legged animal.

Rabbit Warren

A burrow that rabbits make to protect themselves and their offspring.

Reticulum

The second chamber of a ruminant's stomach. It is a crossroad where the particles that enter and leave the rumen are separated. Only small particles of less than a 12th of an inch (2 mm) or dense ones greater than 1 ounce per inch (1.2 g per mm) can go on to the third chamber.

Retina

The inner membrane of the eyes of mammals and other animals, where light sensations are transformed into nerve impulses.

Rod

Along with cones, rods form the photoreceptor cells of the retina of vertebrates. They are responsible for peripheral and night vision, though they perceive colors poorly.

Rumen

The first chamber of a ruminant's stomach. It is a large fermentation vessel that can hold up to 220-265 pounds (100-120 kg) of matter in the process of being digested. Fiber particles remain there between 20 and 48 hours.

Ruminate

The process of chewing food a second time, returning food to the mouth that was already in the chamber that certain animals (ruminants) have.

Scapula

Triangular bone, also called the shoulder blade. With the clavicle, it forms the scapular belt.

Scavenger

Animals that eat organic forms of life that have died. They help maintain the equilibrium of the ecosystem by feeding upon dead animals, breaking them down.

Spermaceti

A waxy substance contained in the organ that bears the same name, located in the head of the sperm whale. It is believed that it aids deep dives, although some specialists believe that it may assist echolocation.

Spinal Cord

An extension of the central nervous system. Often protected by vertebrae, this soft, fatty material is the major nerve pathway that carries information to and from the brain and muscles.

Synapsids

These are also known as therapsids and are described as mammal-like reptiles. They are a class of amniotes that were characterized by a single opening in the cranium (fenestra) behind each eye in the temple. They lived 320 million years ago, during the late Carboniferous Period. It is believed that modern mammals evolved from them.

Tapetum Lucidum

A layer of cells located behind the retina of some vertebrates that reflects light toward the retina, increasing the intensity of the light it receives. It heightens the perception of light in near-darkness.

Trichromatic

Refers to mammals whose eyes have three classes of cones—sensitive to red, green, or blue.

Trophic Chain

System formed by a group of living beings that successively feed on each other.

Udder

Saclike organ containing the mammary glands of certain female mammals.

Ungulate

A mammal that supports itself and walks on the tips of its digits, which are covered by a hoof.

Uropatagium

The membrane that bats have between their feet. It also encloses the tail.

Viviparous

Refers to animals in which the embryonic development of offspring occurs inside the mother's body and the offspring emerge as viable young at birth.

Vomeronasal Organ

An auxiliary organ of the sense of smell located in the vomer bone between the nose and the mouth. Sensory neurons detect different chemical compounds, usually consisting of large molecules.

Warren

A burrow where certain animals raise their young.

Weaning

The process by which a mammal ceases to receive maternal milk as its subsistence.

Whiskers

Very sensitive hairs of many mammals. They are often located near the mouth, like a mustache.

Index